W9-AZK-454

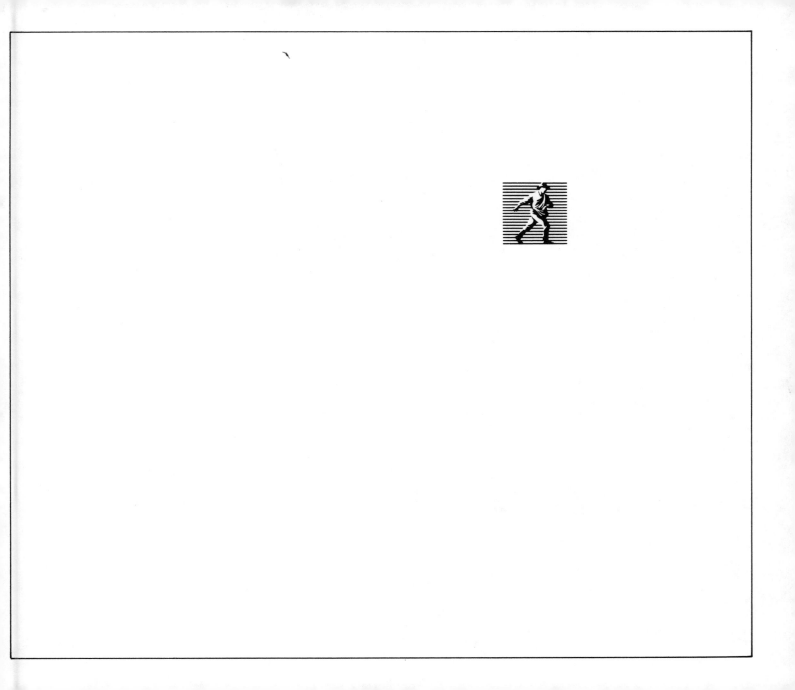

THE BACK OF THE BOX GOURMET

Michael McLaughlin

A John Boswell Associates/King Hill Productions Book

SIMON AND SCHUSTER
New York • London • Toronto • Sydney • Tokyo • Singapore

A John Boswell Associates/King Hill Productions Book

SIMON AND SCHUSTER
Simon & Schuster Building
Rockefeller Center
1230 Avenue of the Americas
New York, New York 10020

Copyright © 1991 by Michael McLaughlin, John Boswell Management, Inc.,
and King Hill Productions.

All rights reserved
including the right of reproduction
in whole or in part in any form.

SIMON AND SCHUSTER and colophon are registered trademarks
of Simon & Schuster Inc.

Printed and bound in the United States of America

5 7 9 10 8 6 4

Library of Congress Cataloging in Publication Data
McLaughlin, Michael.
The back of the box gourmet / by Michael McLaughlin.
p.   cm.
"A John Boswell Associates/King Hill Productions book."
ISBN: 0-671-72356-1
1. Cookery.   I. Title
TX714.M384   1990

641.5--dc20   90-39622
                                                    CIP

For the McLaughlins, the Millers, and all the other
branches of the clan

CONTENTS

INTRODUCTION: CONFESSIONS OF A BACK OF THE BOX GOURMET

I confess to the "crime" of being a gourmet. In my kitchen I stock three different kinds of olive oil. I have a favorite brand of sun-dried tomato. I order my coffee beans by mail from a faraway place. I own a fish poacher, and I use it. I know how to bone a duck. I have eaten *lapereau de campagne au cidre fermier* ("wild hare cooked in country cider"); I can pronounce *lapereau de campagne au cidre fermier.*

So why am I hungry for Lipton's® Famous California Dip? What causes me to crave Campbell's® Green Bean Bake? How do I explain the Toll House® Cookie crumbs between my typewriter keys? The recipe for the *lapereau* is not, after all, printed on the side of the rabbit, so why do I bake a cookie because the recipe is printed on the bag of chocolate chips? Why should opening a can of condensed soup be the first step in cooking a vegetable side dish? How is it possible that I, who once talked on the telephone with Julia Child, can discuss the relative merits of onion dip made with regular Onion Soup Mix versus that made with Golden Onion Soup Mix? Why do otherwise culinarily creative people wander supermarkets aisles, reading a jar of mayonnaise held with one hand and picking up the ingredients for a batch of Hellman's® Easy Macaroni Salad with the other? Why have simple recipes printed on containers of manufactured food products become a deeply ingrained part of the American popular culture?

An easy answer would be that following a series of sophisticated tests, it was discovered that all these product-based recipes contained a seriously addictive substance, which kept consumers coming back for more. The bad news is, the results from the lab came back negative. The good news is, the only thing habit-forming here is convenience and good eating, with a generous dose of nostalgia.

Not that anyone had nostalgia in mind when they developed these dishes. Product recipes, whether they are printed on the back of the box or otherwise distributed, are intended as simple marketing tools. When they first were introduced a century or so ago, they served in place of a yet-to-be nationwide advertising system and, in effect, reached consumers one by one as they picked up the box, can or carton from the store shelf.

There is something uniquely American about this process. It implies a complete faith in the ability of the industrial revolution and the products it generated to improve our lives—usually by shortening the time spent on a tedious chore. From the automobile to Hamburger Helper, entrepreneurs have sought to save us minutes and make a buck along the way. Much of this pioneering spirit has been spent trying to reduce time in the kitchen, and while it would be risky to credit something like canned soup with the beginnings of women's liberation, such advances are an important part of the larger picture, a picture today of a country freed of at least some of its domestic drudgery, and of a society with more time to spend on leisure activities.

Some of these convenience food products, like dried soup mixes, need recipes to explain how to use them; others, like cereal, though they have an obvious function, can be cleverly turned into something else. Like a kind of culinary Swiss Army knife, certain simple food products can become any one of a number of tasty dishes, thus broadening their appeal and making them ever more essential to our pantries. Why settle for selling only a breakfast cereal, when that cereal also makes a delicious party snack?

For major food conglomerates, developing such product recipes is now a full-time industry. Their test kitchens, staffed by diligent home economists and registered dieticians, turn out hundreds, sometimes thousands of recipes yearly. Most are simple, so that the product is the star. All are thoroughly researched, tested and tasted. Most, in fact, are also eminently forgettable, serving their purpose merely by continually reminding us that there's more than one thing to do with oatmeal, or vanilla cookies, or ketchup.

Only a few of these recipes have that intangible quality that makes a genuine classic. But when such magic occurs, food that was intended to be merely convenient becomes something much more important. Such successes are completely unpredictable (test kitchens are continually amazed by the hits), but their effects are undeniable. At Campbell's®, for example, 80 percent of their best-selling condensed soup (Cream of Mushroom) is used not as soup, but as an ingredient in product recipes—green bean casseroles, meat loaves and the like. Thanks to the inevitable emotional influence of food, such classics have also become nostalgic favorites of millions. The best of them endure, are occasionally updated and revised, are continually requested and are cooked in millions of homes every day. When they disappear from boxes, panic ensues. Infrequently, new favorites enter the recipe underground, spreading by eager word of mouth, copied down and passed along, a sign they are already on their way to classic status.

Taken together, the most popular of these back-of-the-box recipes provide a kind of unofficial record of one branch of recent American cookery, and it is rare, indeed, to find someone who isn't inordinately fond of at least one of the recipes in this collection. Sure, I make my own pasta and use fresh herbs abundantly and crave the occasional bite of wild mushroom, caviar and smoked salmon. Food *is* important to me, but none more so than that which I ate growing up. Thus I also crave such back-of-the-package classics as the meat loaf from the Quaker® Oats box, the peanut butter cookies supplied by Skippy® and the so-called nacho dip printed on the Velveeta® carton. If I am now intensely serious about what I eat, that seriousness was formed years ago every time I sat down with my family to share a meal, one that more often than not included one of the recipes in this book.

Perhaps you cook many of these dishes regularly. Possibly you make them only on occasion, when an overwhelming nostalgia knocks thoughts of more sophisticated food right out of your head. Or, sadly, perhaps you haven't thought of these comfortable old foods in years. Whichever is the case, they are collected here for you to cook if you wish, to smile over if you will, to recall and perhaps to rediscover. Whenever you sampled them last, rest assured. They taste as good as ever.

A FEW WORDS
ABOUT THE RECIPES

The texts of the recipes in this book were
provided to me by the corporations that
developed them, and they are printed verbatim.
If these versions do not agree precisely with
your memories, please note that even classic
back-of-the-box formulas are occasionally
revised, usually in response to repeated consumer
input. Under the heading "Gilding the Lily" I
have suggested possible changes (I hesitate to
call them improvements) that you may wish
to investigate. These are my own personal
tamperings, and are included because of my
inability to leave well enough alone. Please feel
free to utilize them or ignore them as you wish.

SNACKTIME: DIPS, DUNKS, APPETIZERS AND HORS D'OEUVRES

Americans munch. We're busy people, always on the go, and eating, like so much else that we do, is frequently accomplished at about 60 miles an hour—whether there's a vehicle involved or not. Such speedy snacks keep us going and provide a little pleasure along the way. They also have inspired a serious collection of back-of-the-box recipes.

The urge to dip, dunk, spread or crunch is not confined to the daily grind, of course, and at home, with your feet up in front of a warm VCR, that same restless need to nibble reasserts itself. Packaged munchies would seem to be unbeatably convenient, but those who develop recipes for the backs of boxes have not given up the fight. Indeed, they seem to have turned the chip, nut and cracker makers' own guns against them, using their products as the building blocks for a collection of delicious snacks that have made the transition from private to public munching and now show up just as frequently when company is on the way. If it's quick and easy enough for everyday but tasty enough for guests, it's surely destined to become a back-of-the-box classic.

THE FAMOUS LIPTON® CALIFORNIA DIP RECIPE

Who has not at one time succumbed to the hypnotic pleasure of this way of life in a bowl, with chips? It may seem as if America has been whipping up this dip for centuries, but in fact it's a relatively new back-of-the-box formulation, which first appeared on Lipton's® Onion Recipe Soup Mix circa 1963. When my pajama-clad brothers and I were small, huddled at the top of the stairs listening to mysterious adult partying below, "onion dip" seemed the height of grown-up sophistication. Later, when the three of us were allowed to hold our own ersatz parties while our parents were away at the real thing, the dip (plus smoked oysters, olives and cubes of cheddar cheese on toothpicks, washed down with 7-UP) was always on the menu.

This imagined *savoir faire* was based on our childish sense that dips (particularly onion soup dip) were what grown-up celebrants ate while having a good time. I don't remember ever calling it California dip, by the way, but even so, there was about it a West Coast casual, drinks-and-barbecue-on-the-deck-in-pedal-pushers aura that contributed to the mystique. Thus it came as a small shock to learn that the dried onion soup and sour cream combination was named merely to honor the California homemaker who first tipped Lipton® to its possibilities some 30 years ago.

Since it fits so neatly together, taking exactly 1 envelope of soup mix and 1 pint-size carton of sour cream, it is also surprising to learn that it took quite a lot of tasting and testing for Lipton® to come up with those precise proportions. So much effort went into the recipe, in fact, that Lipton's® New Jersey neighborhood ran out of sour cream—then a relatively little-known and somewhat scarce product used mostly by Middle European immigrants.

Times change. Nowadays sour cream is a commonplace ingredient, dehydrated soup mixes are big business, and California dip has entered the American lexicon. Sophistication, too, is not as simple a thing as it once was. A batch of onion dip—as easy to stir together as ever—makes me feel quite the opposite of grown up and sophisticated. Though the recipe is always on the Lipton® box (as well as that of rival soup mixers), in the interest of thoroughness I include it here anyway.

In small bowl, blend 1 envelope LIPTON® Onion Recipe Soup Mix with 1 pint (16 oz.) sour cream; chill. Makes about 2 cups dip. For a creamier dip, add more sour cream.

Be creative . . . try adding crumbled bleu cheese or chopped cooked seafood for a delicious variation. Tastes terrific!

GILDING THE LILY: While the point of any back-of-the-box recipe is speed, letting the dip chill for a couple of hours or so and stirring it occasionally will result in a smoother, better-tasting result. The terminally hasty can speed things up by stirring in a tablespoon or two of milk or cream.

SPINACH DIP

The best back-of-the-box formulas enter the national unconscious suddenly, like lightning striking simultaneously across the land and changing forever the way we look at a food product. This spinach dip from Knorr® is perhaps the finest example. At some point in the early 1970s it didn't exist; that same night it was apparently beamed into sleeping brains around the country, and the next day 100,000 or so people prepared it and claimed the recipe for their own.

The test kitchen and publicity people at Knorr® have been amazed for years by the dip's pervasive popularity. Not only does everyone serve it; everyone seems to think they invented it. It has been spotted on the hors d'oeuvre table at a chic New York party, presented by a caterer who haughtily refused to divulge the secret of "his" specialty. The newspaper of record has printed the recipe as one "created" at the country's most prestigious culinary institute. Over several years, dozens of friends have cornered one publicist and pressed the recipe into her hand, claiming it as their own (or their mother's or their best friend's) and suggesting that if Knorr® wanted to use it to promote their products, permission was gladly granted. From around the country, letters to Knorr® have echoed this same willingness to share a private "invention" for the culinary good of the whole.

Even Knorr® isn't sure where the recipe came from (perhaps it was beamed to them at the same time as to the rest of us). One vague tale credits a gourmet catering emporium in the Minneapolis-St. Paul area, but there are few specifics. The only certainty is that the spinach concoction is usually served in a hollowed-out loaf of bread (because it's so ugly otherwise, according to one brutally honest fan). I know you know it (everyone knows it), but here is the recipe anyway. Actually, *I* created it one night when unexpected guests showed up, and all I had in the house was a box of soup mix and a package of frozen spinach.

1	cup HELLMANN'S® Real Mayonnaise
1½	cups sour cream
1	pkg. (10 oz) frozen chopped spinach, thawed, drained
1	pkg. (1.4 oz) KNORR® Vegetable Soup and Recipe Mix
1	can (8 oz) water chestnuts, drained, chopped (optional)
3	green onions, chopped

Stir all ingredients until well mixed. Cover; chill. Serve in hollowed-out loaf of bread. Makes 3 cups.

TRADITIONAL CHEX® BRAND PARTY MIX

¼	cup (½ stick) margarine or butter
1¼	teaspoons seasoned salt
4½	teaspoons Worcestershire sauce
8	cups of your favorite CHEX® Brand Cereals (Corn, Rice and/or Wheat)
1	cup salted mixed nuts
1	cup pretzel sticks

Preheat oven to 250°. In open roasting pan melt margarine in oven. Stir in seasoned salt and Worcestershire sauce. Gradually add cereals, nuts and pretzels, stirring until all pieces are evenly coated. Bake 1 hour, stirring every 15 minutes. Spread on absorbent paper to cool. Stir in airtight container.

Makes 9 cups

One of my grandmothers was a glorious cook, the kind who made bacon, eggs and hashed browns just to kill time while a batch of her sweet rolls was baking. If there were only two kinds of homemade jam on the table, she apologized, and if the main course were roast chicken, she frequently glazed a ham—just in case. The other grandmother also cooked, but she hated the process and never voluntarily made anything—except this ubiquitous crunchy cereal snack, for which she was locally famous.

Each year at Christmas she turned out prodigious mountains of snack mix, stirred together in an enormous turkey roaster. Everyone got a Christmas paper-decorated tin of the stuff, and everyone fought for the cashews she insisted were the secret of its excellence. She called it "TV Mix," and her version came not from a Chex® box but from the competition's. Otherwise it was virtually identical to the official Chex® formula, one that first made the party rounds in St. Louis as early as 1955, where it was created by Ralston Purina Company.

HOT ARTICHOKE DIP

I remember the precise moment I first really appreciated mayonnaise. I was a guest of fellow college students, and the appetizer of a rather stark student meal consisted of hot, barely cooked spears of fresh broccoli dipped into nothing more than Hellmann's® mayo. Brought up on "salad dressing" (the house brand was Miracle Whip), I found the tart, smooth stuff a revelation. I had never thought of mayonnaise as a sauce, and it had certainly never occurred to me as something worth eating except in a sandwich.

All this is by way of attempting to justify the appeal of the popular hot spread below. It is of uncertain origin, but because the formula is so easy to remember and the dip so easy to make, it is wildly popular. Also, like many of the best back-of-the-box recipes, the components are nonperishable pantry staples—great for short-notice partying. Though this recipe cuts the mayonnaise with sour cream, ultra-stylish artichokes remain the center of attention, and of the several versions I have sampled, this is the tastiest. Rye bread squares or crackers are commonly called for, but around the country regional substitutions, such as toasted pita bread triangles or corn tortilla chips, are also enjoyed.

½ cup HELLMANN'S® or BEST FOODS® Real Mayonnaise
½ cup sour cream
1 can (14 oz) artichoke hearts, drained, chopped
⅓ cup grated Parmesan cheese
⅛ teaspoon hot pepper sauce

Stir all ingredients until well mixed. Spoon into small ovenproof dish. Bake at 350°F 30 minutes or until bubbly. Makes 2 cups.

GILDING THE LILY: Marinated artichokes, well-drained, can be substituted.

HOT CRABMEAT APPETIZER

Again no date of origin is known for this hors d'oeuvre, but it has been a staple on the party circuit for years. It is a cousin of the artichoke concoction above, and they often show up at parties together.

1	8-oz. pkg. PHILADELPHIA BRAND Cream Cheese
1½	cups (7½-oz. can) flaked drained crabmeat
2	tablespoons finely chopped onion
2	tablespoons milk
½	teaspoon KRAFT Cream Style Horseradish
¼	teaspoon salt
	Dash of pepper
⅓	cup sliced almonds, toasted

Combine softened cream cheese, crabmeat, onion, milk, horseradish and seasonings, mixing until well blended. Spoon into 9-inch pie plate or oven-proof dish; sprinkle with nuts. Bake at 375°, 15 minutes. Serve as a dip or spread with crackers, chips or raw vegetables.

Variation: An 8-oz. can of clams and a sprinkle of dill are excellent alternatives for the crabmeat and almonds.

GILDING THE LILY: Though developed before the days of surimi, this recipe is as good a place as any to opt for one of the several pseudo-seafoods on the market. Sliced green onions can be substituted for the regular sort. The horseradish and pepper can be increased, to taste.

CLASSIC NACHO DIP

In medium saucepan, cook onions in margarine; reduce heat to low.

Add remaining ingredients; stir until process cheese spread is melted.

Serve hot with tortilla chips or vegetable dippers. 3 cups

PREP TIME: 10 minutes   COOKING TIME: 10 minutes

GILDING THE LILY: Use green onions in place of regular onions. Cook a generous pinch of oregano with the onions. For extra fire, add minced pickled jalapeños to taste. For an important flavor boost, sprinkle the top of the dip with toasted whole cumin seeds just before serving.

Chile con queso is an unctuously orange, piquantly gooey hot cheese dip that represents the essence of tacky but tasty Tex-Mex food. Based on (but resembling not at all) a genuine Mexican appetizer of the same name, it is at its simple best when made with American process cheese. Of course the zesty pairing of melted cheese and hot peppers, scooped onto a waiting corn chip and into an eager mouth, inevitably invites comparison with that other Tex-Mex bar snack, nachos. Nowadays, nachos are, in fact, often nothing more than tortilla chips slathered with molten jalapeño cheese sauce (look for them at the airport, the baseball stadium or even the movie theater), and the line between them and chile con queso is growing blurry, hence the slightly misleading title of this excellent, easy version from Kraft. Who cares what it's called?

2	tablespoons PARKAY Margarine
½	cup chopped onion
1	lb. VELVEETA Mexican Pasteurized Process Cheese Spread with Jalapeño Pepper, cubed
1	14½-oz. can tomatoes, chopped, drained Tortilla chips or vegetable dippers

SWEET 'N' SOUR MEATBALLS

No chapter of snack cuisine would be complete without something served hot from a chafing dish, or on a toothpick—or both. To relive the pleasure of spearing the meaty morsels and to once again know the joy of maneuvering one of the drippy little things into your mouth without damage to carpeting, frock or necktie is to reaffirm why chafing dishes were once so popular. For the hostess, of course, sweet and sour meatballs could be completed conveniently well in advance. For guests, however, the chafing dish and its messy meatballs represented a kind of socially acceptable game of "chicken," with the winner's prize the lowest dry-cleaning bill. If you still own a chafing dish (it's probably in the attic, next to the fondue pot), these savory little meatballs, swimming in a piquant chili sauce and currant jelly mixture, are a perfect reason to dust it off and fire it up. Now, where in the world is the Sterno?

1	pound lean ground beef
1	cup soft bread crumbs
1	egg, slightly beaten
2	tablespoons minced onion
2	tablespoons milk
1	clove garlic, minced
1	teaspoon salt
	Dash pepper
1	tablespoon vegetable oil
⅔	cup HEINZ Chili Sauce
⅔	cup red currant jelly

Combine first 8 ingredients; form into 40 bite-size meatballs, using a full teaspoon for each. Brown meatballs lightly in oil. Cover; simmer 10 minutes. Drain excess fat. Combine chili sauce and jelly; pour over meatballs. Heat, stirring occasionally, until jelly is melted. Simmer 10 to 12 minutes until sauce has thickened; baste occasionally. Makes 40 appetizers (¾ cup sauce).

GILDING THE LILY: A few hearty shakes of the Tabasco bottle will add welcome heat to the fruity sauce.

HIDDEN VALLEY RANCH® OYSTER CRACKERS

Every corporate test kitchen would like to lay claim to a classic as enduring as Chex® Party Mix. Many are called but few are up to the challenge. One upstart with a lot of promise is this tangy, garlicky oyster cracker–based munchie. My father, whose previous kitchen duties mainly consisted of tending the barbecue and cooking any wild game he had hunted (Mom wouldn't touch it), has added this snack to his repertoire. He insists I include it here. Inspired by my grandmother's Party Mix, Dad thinks it needs pretzels and mixed nuts (definitely cashews), but otherwise it is a classic in the making.

12-16 oz. plain oyster crackers
1   pkg. HIDDEN VALLEY RANCH® Buttermilk Recipe Original Ranch Salad Dressing Mix
¼   tsp. lemon pepper
½-1   tsp. dill weed
¼   tsp garlic powder
¾-1   cup salad oil

Combine HIDDEN VALLEY RANCH® mix and oil; add dill weed, garlic powder and lemon pepper. Pour over crackers, stir to coat. Place in warm oven for 15-20 minutes.

GILDING THE LILY: Those who long for mixed nuts and/or pretzels in their snack mix can double the recipe and replace part of the crackers with suitable additions.

ALMOND CHEDDAR PINECONE

16   ounces cream cheese, softened
½   pound cheddar cheese, grated
6   tablespoons port
⅛   teaspoon cayenne
¼   cup finely sliced green onion
2   cups BLUE DIAMOND® Whole Natural or
       Blanched Whole Almonds, toasted
Crackers

Anyone can serve a plain old cheese ball—and probably has. They are usually sculpted from odd cheeses, rolled in chopped nuts to disguise their dubious innards, served up with blind hope and eaten (if at all) with disdain. The inevitable substantial leftovers turn up the next day transformed into everyone's lunchbox cheese (ball) sandwiches. And that's the fresh, homemade version. Just imagine the fate of those boxed cheese balls from the supermarket dairy case!

Despite a childhood fondness for port wine cheddar (and a love of nuts that even today borders on a serious medical problem), the cheese ball always left me unimpressed. It wasn't until I was in college and ran across the Almond Cheddar Pinecone at a catered university event that I admitted it made great party food. A mound of decent cheeses, overlaid with a fool-the-eye application of almonds and garnished with sprigs of fresh pine, it struck me (clutching my plastic glass of Mateus rosé) as the ultimate edible holiday centerpiece. It still does.

Combine first 4 ingredients; beat until smooth. Stir in green onions. Cover and refrigerate one hour. Form cheese mixture into the shape of a large pinecone. Place on serving plate. Beginning at narrow end of cone, carefully press almonds about ¼-inch deep into cheese mixture in rows, making sure that pointed end of each almond extends at a slight angle. Continue pressing almonds into cheese mixture in rows, with rows slightly overlapping, until all cheese is covered. Garnish pinecone with pine sprigs, if desired. Serve with crackers.

Makes about 25 servings

GILDING THE LILY: With the neutral base of cream cheese left unaltered, other cheeses (blue, Swiss, goat cheese) can be substituted. Brandy and garlic can replace port and green onions. To toast almonds, bake them on an ungreased sheet in a 350° oven for 10 to 12 minutes, stirring often, until crisp and browned.

SUPPERS: SUNDAY COMFORT ALL WEEK LONG

Supper—that warm and cozy, end-of-the-day gathering of the family to share a freshly prepared meal—inevitably suffered when mothers went to work outside the home. Many convenience food products, and the back-of-the-box recipes that utilized them, were designed primarily to help working women recreate some semblance of all-day-at-the-stove meals in a minimum amount of time.

In the Nineties, when the husband or one of the kids is as likely as Mom to be in charge of getting dinner on the table, saving time remains no less an issue, and these convenience recipes from the past gain new relevance. Meat loaves and casseroles—elsewhere in this book—are savory solutions, as are the following tried and true back-of-the-box main courses. These recipes can be thrown together quickly, but they have a tender, generous quality that evokes the homemade comfort supper is all about.

CLASSIC GLORIFIED CHICKEN

This saucy chicken dish from Campbell's® is one of the seven best-ever recipes developed by the canned soup folks. For busy people, it is a kind of dream dish, which bakes unattended while the cook (if that is the right word) deals with easy accompaniments like steamed broccoli and white rice. The minimal list of ingredients and complete lack of any rigorous kitchen technique make it the sort of recipe a fretful mother tearfully presses into the hands of a child (particularly a male child) as he moves into his first apartment. Newlyweds, too, eat plenty of Glorified Chicken and since there are several possible types of canned soup that can be dumped over the baking bird (each one producing a slightly different result), the marriage can be several months old before the culinary honeymoon ends.

fresh mush. - slice - add to
chick 20 min after
putting in oven

add ½ c white wine + rosemary
to crm of mush soup

2½-3   pound broiler-fryer chicken, cut up
2   tablespoons butter or margarine
1   can (10¾ ounces) CAMPBELL'S® Condensed Cream of Chicken Soup

1. In 12- by 8-inch baking dish, arrange chicken skin-side up. Drizzle with butter. Bake at 375°F. for 40 minutes.

2. Spoon soup over chicken. Bake 20 minutes more or until chicken is fork-tender. Stir sauce before serving. Makes 4 servings.

GILDING THE LILY: Add 3 tablespoons medium-dry sherry to the soup when spooned over the chicken. Substitute Cream of Mushroom, Cheddar Cheese or Cream of Celery Soup. Add minced pickled jalapeño peppers and sliced green olives to the cheese soup version. Add chopped pimiento to the celery or mushroom variations. Add ½ teaspoon dried tarragon or basil to the chicken soup variation.

BAKED SPAM® LUNCHEON MEAT

SPAM® Luncheon Meat, produced by Hormel, fed many a soldier but managed to survive wartime with more of its reputation intact than did that other military staple, chipped dried beef. America shared SPAM® with its Allies, and Khrushchev is said to have reminisced that the "luncheon loaf" helped feed the entire Russian army, a last homey touch of *glasnost* before the Cold War set in. Perhaps its low cost and astonishing seven-year shelf life have something to do with the enduring popularity of this canned ham and pork combination, which has been around for over 50 years.

While it can be sliced and served cold, in sandwiches and salads, or sautéed or broiled (great with breakfast eggs), SPAM® is at its most appealingly retro when baked in a loaf and glazed with a mixture of mustard, vinegar and brown sugar. Pictured on the can studded with whole cloves just like a Sunday ham (an oddly ornate treatment for the squatty little block of meat), the glazed loaf makes a quick supper main course, and along with the heating up of the cream of tomato soup, comprised my first real kitchen skills.

Score top and dot with cloves. BAKE at 375°F. for 35 minutes. Baste with mixture of ⅓ cup brown sugar, ½ tsp. vinegar, 1 tsp. prepared mustard and 1 tsp. water.

GILDING THE LILY: The sweet glaze offers a fine contrast to the salty meat. Double the glaze if you like, and use more mustard, to taste. The loaf can also be sliced, and the individual slices glazed and baked, which speeds up the process somewhat.

BAKED CHICKEN PARMESAN

Except for the chicken, all the ingredients in this quick main course are cupboard staples, making it easy to shop for and simple to prepare. Once again the magic of mayonnaise (remember when it was recommended as a hair conditioner?) inspires some very good eating and results in moist chicken beneath a crusty corn flake crust.

1	2½ to 3-lb. broiler-fryer, cut up, skinned
¾	cup KRAFT Real Mayonnaise or MIRACLE WHIP Salad Dressing
1	cup corn flake crumbs
½	cup (2 ozs.) KRAFT 100% Grated Parmesan Cheese
	Dash of salt and pepper

Preheat oven to 350°.

Mix crumbs and Parmesan cheese.

Brush chicken with mayonnaise; coat with crumbs. Sprinkle with salt and pepper.

Place in 13 × 9-inch baking dish. Bake 1 hour or until tender. 3 to 4 servings.

PREP TIME: 15 minutes   COOKING TIME: 1 hour

OLD-FASHIONED POT ROAST

Pot roast is the ideal Sabbath day meal. I was only 10 when I realized it took exactly the same length of time for a tough cut of meat to cook to melting tenderness as it did for Sunday school and church services to run their stately course. Walking into a house full of the rich smells of an almost-ready pot roast simmering away in the oven was my boyhood reward for not squirming too much during the last hymn. We said grace only when company was present, but I was thankful every time pot roast was on the menu.

Nowadays, most of us feel the ideal meal should take no longer to prepare than the 10 minutes or so in which pasta or a boneless chicken breast cooks. A dish that demands several hours is no longer a common event, even when those hours don't require the cook's constant attention. Sometimes, though, the mood strikes, and when you want the mellow, oniony flavors of a well-cooked pot roast, this recipe from Lipton® will at least minimize the preparation time. The simplified results (don't forget to serve plenty of mashed potatoes and other fixings) will also deliver a comfortable Sunday kind of satisfaction—one you'll be genuinely thankful for.

3-3½ pound boneless pot roast (rump, chuck or round)
1 envelope LIPTON® Onion, Beefy Onion, Beefy Mushroom or Onion-Mushroom Recipe Soup Mix
2¼ cups water

In Dutch oven, brown roast. Add LIPTON® Onion Recipe Soup Mix blended with water. Simmer covered, turning occasionally, 2½ hours or until tender. If desired, thicken gravy. Makes about 6 servings.

Try some of these delicious international variations:

French-Style Pot Roast—Decrease water to 1¼ cups. Add 1 cup dry red wine and 1 teaspoon thyme.

German-Style Pot Roast—Decrease water to ¾ cup. Add 1½ cups beer, 1 teaspoon brown sugar and ½ teaspoon caraway seeds.

Italian-Style Pot Roast—Decrease water to 1 cup. Add 1 can (14½ oz.) whole tomatoes, drained, 1 teaspoon basil and 1 bay leaf.

OVEN-FRIED CHICKEN

Here is another unattended entree, one that eliminates standing over a hot stove. For the cook feeding a family at the end of a long day, this means there's at least a reasonable expectation of sitting down on the job. The dish rearranges chicken and potatoes—natural suppertime partners—into something a little clever and quirky. The chicken's crisp herb-and-potato flake coating is so easy and quick, you'll even have time to make real mashed potatoes by way of accompaniment.

1	cup HUNGRY JACK® Mashed Potato Flakes
1	teaspoon salt
¼	teaspoon pepper
¼	teaspoon rosemary, crushed
¼	to ½ teaspoon poultry seasoning
1	egg, slightly beaten
1	teaspoon lemon juice
2½-3	lb. frying chicken, cut up

Heat oven to 375°F. In plastic bag, combine potato flakes and seasonings. In shallow bowl, combine egg and lemon juice. Dip chicken pieces in egg mixture; shake in plastic bag. Place chicken skin-side-up in ungreased 15 × 10-inch jelly roll pan. Bake, uncovered, at 375°F. for 60 to 75 minutes or until chicken is tender. 6 servings.

MEAT LOAVES: MEAT LOAF MADNESS

Meat loaves—rich, moist, tender and simple—are suddenly turning up on the menus of chi-chi restaurants from coast to coast. This so-called renaissance is part of something dubbed The Diner Movement, and while I can't explain the retro appeal of reindeer sweaters, Naugahyde sling chairs or "The Brady Bunch," rediscovering meat loaf makes perfect sense. Consider: After a tough day at the office, who wants food that takes an atlas or a biology text to identify? Meat loaf has no mysterious bones, it can be smothered in ketchup without embarrassment, and seconds (remember seconds?) won't cost you another $32. Meat loaf hasn't been wok-charred, fanned out on oversized plates, napped with *beurre blanc* or grilled over anything. If it has, send it back, and make your own meat loaf at home.

Sure meat loaf is a comfort to eat, but it's also a comfort to cook. The chi-chi restaurants will eventually move on to another trend, but meat loaves will stay in vogue (if not in *Vogue*) because they are so accommodating to prepare. A bowl, a pan, maybe a knife and a spoon, are all it takes. In fact, getting your hands into the bowl, which is really the best way to mix the meat, provides the kind of physical therapy that any number of wild-mushroom-and-lobster-stuffed ravioli recipes can't; and it eliminates a spoon to wash. Cooking meat loaf as a step toward achieving stress reduction and improved mental health may be a modern notion, but most of the best meat loaf recipes have been around for years. Here are four of my favorites.

RED MAGIC MEAT LOAF

Ketchup in and ketchup on keeps the meat loaf moist and flavorful. This classic from Heinz also includes an odd but tasty touch of pineapple—especially nice if you include a bit of ground pork in place of some of the beef.

1½   pounds lean ground beef
1   cup soft bread crumbs
⅓   cup HEINZ Tomato Ketchup
¼   cup chopped onion
1   egg, slightly beaten
½   teaspoon salt
⅛   teaspoon pepper
¼   cup HEINZ Tomato Ketchup
¼   cup drained crushed pineapple

Combine first 7 ingredients. Form into a loaf (8″ × 4″ × 1-½″) in shallow baking pan. Bake in 350°F oven, 40 minutes. Remove from oven; combine remaining ¼ cup ketchup with pineapple and spoon over top of loaf. Return loaf to oven; bake an additional 30 minutes. Let meat loaf stand 5 minutes before slicing. Makes 6 servings.

GILDING THE LILY: This meat loaf could use a touch more pepper. Replace about one-third of the beef with ground pork (not too lean, not too fat) in any of these meat loaves for a moister, better-tasting result.

PRIZE-WINNING MEAT LOAF

Jokes are made about meat loaves that are all filler, but the truth is, to prevent the loaf from being too heavy and dense, a modest measure of extender is needed. Crushed crackers, bread crumbs and corn flakes all work well, and all have their fans. Rolled oats, readily at hand in diners and coffee shops, seem particularly successful, and this recipe is a favorite of many a beanery chef. Old as it is (it's appeared on Quaker® Oats boxes for years), the trendiness of oat bran, a major component of rolled oats, makes the formula seem brand new—and may even justify a second helping.

1	cup tomato juice
¾	cup QUAKER® Oats (quick or old fashioned, uncooked)
1	egg, beaten (optional)
¼	cup chopped onion
1	teaspoon salt (optional)
¼	teaspoon pepper
1½	lb. lean ground beef

Heat oven to 350°F. Combine all ingredients except ground beef; mix well. Add ground beef; mix lightly but thoroughly. Press into 8 × 4-inch loaf pan; bake 1 hour. Let stand 5 minutes before slicing.

8 SERVINGS

GILDING THE LILY: This loaf won't be harmed if the amounts of onion and pepper given are doubled. The healthy heart people have been at the recipe, and while the egg and salt may well be optional, omitting them causes the meat loaf's flavor and texture to suffer; if your cardiologist permits, leave them in.

SOUPERIOR MEAT LOAF

No matter how tender and moist it is, a bland and under-seasoned meat loaf will always taste like institutional fare. One typical solution to meat loaf ennui is plenty of minced onion, plus a splash of beef broth for added richness. By printing this recipe on their soup mix box, Lipton® does most of the work, allowing you to skip arduous onion peeling and chopping. The resulting loaf (as well as the mushroom alternative) is flavorful indeed.

1	envelope LIPTON® Onion, Beefy Onion or Beefy Mushroom Recipe Soup Mix
2	pounds ground beef
1½	cups soft bread crumbs
2	eggs
¾	cup water
⅓	cup ketchup

Preheat oven to 350°.

In large bowl, combine all ingredients. In large shallow baking pan, shape into loaf. Bake 1 hour or until done. Makes about 8 servings.

GILDING THE LILY: Perfect though it is, this loaf could use a generous grinding of fresh black pepper.

CLASSIC FAMILY MEAT LOAF

Good Enough to Eat, a homey restaurant on Manhattan's Upper West Side, makes a meat loaf of considerable renown. Co-owner Carrie Levin, who along with partner Ann Nickinson has collected the restaurant's recipes into a cookbook, confesses her meat loaf's secret touch is a can of condensed Campbell's® soup—Cream of Tomato or Golden Mushroom, take your choice. For publication, Nickinson and Levin (who even served the meat loaf at her wedding) tried recreating the taste and moist texture with ingredients more suitably "cookbook-ish" than canned soup. After much effort (and ground beef) they admitted failure, and they no longer blush at the short cut—one that the Campbell® people have long known makes a great meat loaf. The official Campbell® recipe even includes a simple gravy. Pass the potatoes, please.

1	can (10¾ ounces) CAMPBELL'S® Condensed Cream of Mushroom or Tomato Soup
1½	pounds ground beef
½	cup fine dry bread crumbs
¼	cup finely chopped onion
1	tablespoon Worcestershire sauce
1	egg, beaten
⅛	teaspoon pepper
¼	cup water

1. In large bowl, mix *thoroughly* ½ cup of the soup, beef, bread crumbs, onion, Worcestershire, egg and pepper. In 12- by 8-inch baking pan, *firmly* shape meat into 8- by 4-inch loaf.

2. Bake at 350°F. for 1¼ hours or until done. Spoon off fat, reserving 1 to 2 tablespoons drippings.

3. In 1-quart saucepan over medium heat, heat remaining soup, water and reserved drippings to boiling, stirring occasionally. Serve sauce with meat loaf. Makes 6 servings.

GILDING THE LILY: Increase the onion to at least ½ cup; season generously with freshly ground black pepper. This loaf, and the three above, might welcome ⅓ to ½ cup finely diced sweet green or red pepper. There is not enough of the savory little gravy to go very far, but it is easily doubled (or tripled, to avoid partial cans of opened soup) if you wish. For added richness, substitute milk for the water in the gravy.

CASSEROLES: AMERICA'S ONE-POT LOVE AFFAIR

Somewhere M. F. K. Fisher, the grande dame of American food writers, has written sensitively and amusingly about casseroles. It would be nice if those of us who grew up in the Fifties and Sixties could find such significant insights into the human condition bubbling beneath that ominous crust. Instead, most will greet the casserole with suspicion. We know now—as we knew then—that such suppers will be filling and thus give, when tucked away in the belly, comfort of a sort. Unfortunately, we also recall that most casseroles were quick and inexpensive for Mom to concoct and often featured veteran surviving ingredients from one or more previous meals. As grown-ups we find it difficult to feel nostalgic for—or hunger after—any dish, however filling, whose major plusses are that it is "inexpensive," "leftover" or "quick."

Such murky casserole disasters are caused (as Fisher points out) by impetuous improvisation fired by economic desperation. One cannot, after all, expect to combine four or five totally unrelated food groups under a blanket of canned soup, cheese and crushed potato chips and produce anything more than fodder.

Still, there is hope. Though rare, a well-planned casserole is always possible, and its appeal to hungry people is undeniable. Moms and others with crowds to feed at the end of the day had better leave improvisation to The Actors' Studio, and turn to the back of the box, where, among the classic foolproof casseroles, the four that follow stand out as exceptional.

CLASSIC TUNA NOODLE CASSEROLE

This recipe defines the American casserole. Every other Friday (fish sticks alternated) it was school cafeteria fare, and I welcomed it for the rich, gooey quality that was lacking in Monday through Thursday's sensible entrees. Inevitably, even though the week's lunch program menu was printed in the town paper in advance, there were scheduling snafus, and it was possible to come home after a lunch of tuna noodle casserole to find a supper of tuna noodle casserole. Mom only had three (not 300) kids to feed, but she could be forgiven for sharing the lunch program's enthusiasm for this recipe that so easily fills up the hungriest of crowds. Only my father protested, meowing loudly as he came in the door, but he cleaned his plate like the rest of us.

Who better than Campbell's® to supply the recipe? For years their classic was given as Tuna Casserole. It was without noodles, and there were sliced hard-cooked eggs, making it stark fare indeed. Today's Campbell® classic adds welcome pasta and a stylish topping of browned bread crumbs, and it is as good—maybe better—than any you ever ate in the lunchroom.

Campbell's®

1	can (10 ¾ ounces) CAMPBELL'S® Condensed Cream of Celery Soup
½	cup milk
2	cups cooked medium egg noodles (2 cups uncooked)
1	cup cooked peas
2	tablespoons chopped pimento
2	cans (about 7 ounces *each*) tuna, drained and flaked
1	tablespoon butter or margarine
2	tablespoons fine dry bread crumbs

1. In 1½-quart casserole, combine soup and milk. Stir in noodles, peas, pimento and tuna. Bake at 400°F. for 25 minutes or until hot; stir.

2. Meanwhile, in small saucepan over medium heat, in hot butter, stir bread crumbs until lightly browned. Top casserole with bread crumbs; bake 5 minutes more. Makes 4½ cups or 4 servings.

GILDING THE LILY: Use Mushroom Soup in place of the Celery Soup. Use short curly fusilli-type pasta instead of noodles. Frozen peas need not be cooked, only defrosted. The browned bread crumbs are a nice touch, but if you prefer potato chips on your tuna noodle casserole, lightly crush about ½ cup, sprinkle them over the top after stirring, and bake another 5 minutes.

CHILI PIE CASSEROLE

Fritos® brand Corn Chips were created by Texan Elmer Doolin sometime around 1932. Beginning with a formula purchased from a Mexican cook, adapted from the authentic corn tortilla, Doolin parlayed his snack business into a national phenomenon. Fritos® brand Corn Chips chili pie, invented by Doolin's mother, Daisy, is a baked dish of corn chips, chili, onions and cheese that soon became the Southwest's equivalent of the tuna noodle casserole. The Walkabout, created by spooning chili, cheese and onions into an opened snack-size bag of Fritos® brand Corn Chips, is eaten on the hoof with a spoon and is still enjoyed at drive-ins, rodeos, state fairs and the like.

3　　cups FRITOS® brand Corn Chips, divided
1　　large onion, chopped
1　　cup grated American cheese, divided
1　　19-ounce can chili

Spread 2 cups FRITOS® Corn Chips in a baking dish. Arrange chopped onion and half of the cheese on top of the corn chips. Pour chili over onions and cheese. Top with remaining corn chips and cheese. Bake at 350°F. for 15 to 20 minutes or until hot and bubbly. Makes 4 to 6 servings.

GILDING THE LILY: Homemade chili (use about 2½ cups) and sharp cheddar or jalapeño jack cheese will improve the flavor immeasurably. Pass toppings—sour cream, diced tomato, shredded lettuce, guacamole—at the table. This somewhat gooey dish is less messy to serve if baked in individual casseroles or gratin dishes.

IMPOSSIBLE CHEESEBURGER PIE

Bisquick®, developed in the early 1930s to make whipping up a batch of light and tender biscuits a snap, gradually acquired much more influence, as Betty Crocker and company expanded its uses to include pancakes, waffles, muffins, dumplings, as well as appetizers, main courses, vegetable side dishes and hundreds of desserts. All were soon found at one time or another on the Bisquick® box, as it came to the rescue of inexperienced or hurried cooks across the land. Among the most popular of Bisquick's® back-of-the-box lifesavers are the easy casseroles and desserts known as "impossible pies."

They are, obviously, not impossible at all, and Bisquick® boasts cherry, seafood, French apple, ham 'n' swiss, pumpkin, tuna-cheddar, bacon, taco, lasagne, chicken 'n' broccoli and pizza variations. In all of them a Bisquick®-based batter is poured over the filling or combined with it. During the baking, the batter sinks to the bottom and forms a crust— easy kitchen magic of the best kind.

1	pound ground beef
1½	cups chopped onion
½	teaspoon salt
¼	teaspoon pepper
1½	cups milk
¾	cup BISQUICK® Baking Mix
3	eggs
2	tomatoes, sliced
1	cup shredded Cheddar or process American cheese

Heat oven to 400°. Grease pie plate, 10 × 1½ inches. Brown beef and onion; drain. Stir in salt and pepper. Spread in plate. Beat milk, baking mix and eggs until smooth, 15 seconds in blender on high or 1 minute with hand beater. Pour into plate. Bake 25 minutes. Top with tomatoes; sprinkle with cheese. Bake until knife inserted in center comes out clean, 5 to 8 minutes. Cool 5 minutes. 6 to 8 servings.

GILDING THE LILY: Like a cheeseburger on a bun, this will benefit from the best red, ripe and juicy tomatoes you can find.

TASTY TURKEY POT PIE

Pot pies—at least the anonymous frozen ones in those little foil pans—are more suspect than any other prepared foods. After all, if you're eating something hidden under a pastry crust, wouldn't you be happier knowing the cook who did the hiding? Leftovers are one thing, but a major food company's leftovers are simply unacceptable. Make the acquaintance, then, of this simple recipe, which provides a great place to use up leftover portions of the holiday bird or cooked turkey breast and offers a warm, comforting way to end the day. The cook, or a young assistant (this was one of my earliest kitchen chores), even gets the thrill of popping open a can of refrigerated dinner rolls.

½	cup KRAFT MIRACLE WHIP Salad Dressing
2	tablespoons flour
1	teaspoon instant chicken bouillon
⅛	teaspoon pepper
¾	cup milk
1½	cups chopped turkey or chicken
1	10-oz. pkg. frozen mixed vegetables, thawed, drained
1	4-oz. can refrigerated quick crescent dinner rolls

Combine salad dressing, flour, bouillon and pepper in medium saucepan. Gradually add milk. Cook, stirring constantly, over low heat until thickened. Add turkey and vegetables; heat thoroughly, stirring occasionally. Spoon into 8-inch square baking dish. Unroll dough into two rectangles. Press perforations together to seal. Place rectangles side-by-side to form square; press edges together to form seam. Cover turkey mixture with dough. Bake at 375°, 15 to 20 minutes or until browned.

PREPARATION TIME: 15 minutes   BAKING TIME: 20 minutes

GILDING THE LILY: Diced roasted red pepper (pimiento) or minced fresh parsley will add color and freshness to the filling. The pot pie can also be prepared with canned tuna or salmon, or cooked shrimp. The recipe can be doubled. Use a 12 × 8-inch baking dish; top the pot pie with 3 rectangles of crescent roll dough; cut shapes out of the remaining dough and decorate the crust with the cut-outs before baking. A wash of 1 egg beaten with 1 tablespoon cold water, brushed over the dough before baking, will add golden color.

SIDE DISHES: VEGETABLES, POTATOES, SALADS & STUFFING

If it is the little things that make a great meal, success can be as close as the back of the nearest box. While it is possible to buy decent side salads from the deli and to create passable stuffing by adding water to a mix, when supper is as ordinary as a carry-out chicken or as simple as leftover roast beef from the fridge, an accompaniment that is freshly prepared can make the difference between merely eating and actually enjoying.

On the other hand, if the fried chicken is homemade, the baked ham from a pricey smokehouse or the pastrami from Second Avenue's finest deli, it seems only appropriate that the side dishes also be first-rate. Among the most interesting back-of-the-box categories is this eclectic collection of hot vegetables, comforting carbohydrates and tangy salads— all easy ways to round out your menus with convenience and with a kind of genuinely American style that can be achieved no other way.

CRISP ONION-ROASTED POTATOES

At Lipton®, requests for this relatively new recipe are coming in at a remarkable rate—the sure sign of a classic in the making.

1	envelope LIPTON® Onion-Mushroom Recipe Soup Mix
½	cup olive or vegetable oil
¼	cup IMPERIAL® Margarine, melted
1	teaspoon thyme leaves (optional)
1	teaspoon marjoram leaves (optional)
¼	teaspoon pepper
2	pounds all-purpose potatoes, cut into quarters

Preheat oven to 450°.

In shallow baking or roasting pan, thoroughly blend all ingredients except potatoes. Add potatoes and turn to coat thoroughly. Bake, stirring occasionally, 60 minutes or until potatoes are tender and golden brown. Garnish, if desired, with chopped parsley. Makes about 8 servings.

Also terrific with LIPTON® Onion Recipe Soup Mix.

GILDING THE LILY: The potatoes can be left unpeeled. The herbs and the fresh parsley do much to make the dish successful. More pepper won't hurt a thing.

CLASSIC GREEN BEAN BAKE

This is it—one of the seven most popular Campbell® Kitchens product recipes ever, chosen from a field of over 16,000, and perhaps the quintessential back-of-the-box formula. For a generation or two of Americans, this is what "eat your vegetables" meant, and for a generation or two of potluck suppers, church sociables and other communal gatherings, this uncomplicated casserole was easily the most familiar dish on the table. Of the 325 million cans of Cream of Mushroom Soup Campbell's® sells every year, over 80 percent are used for sauces, most of them, I'll wager, in this classic vegetable side dish.

There are some surprises in this most current version. For example, I can't imagine my mother (or those millions of other average American cooks of the Fifties and Sixties) having a bottle of soy sauce in the house, and I always thought the addition of onion rings was the invention of a wacky neighbor of ours back in Colorado. Otherwise the recipe tastes the same as it always did and goes together with the sort of simplicity that made it—and still makes it—such a welcome addition to so many different meals.

1	can (10¾ ounces) CAMPBELL'S® Condensed Cream of Mushroom Soup
½	cup milk
1	teaspoon soy sauce
	Dash pepper
4	cups cooked green beans
1	can (2.8 ounces) French fried onions

1. In 1½-quart casserole, combine soup, milk, soy and pepper. Stir in green beans and ½ can onions.
2. Bake at 350°F. for 25 minutes or until hot; stir. Top with remaining onions. Bake 5 minutes more. Makes about 4 cups, 8 servings.

TIP: Buy 2 packages (9 ounces *each*) frozen cut green beans, 2 cans (about 16 ounces *each*) cut green beans or about 1½ pounds fresh green beans for this recipe.

GILDING THE LILY: For a crunchier texture, substitute French-cut green beans, thawed and drained but otherwise uncooked. Shoestring potato sticks (do they still exist?), sliced almonds, packaged croutons or cubes of fresh white bread can be used on top—but not stirred into—the beans. Add them about halfway through the cooking process and bake until lightly browned.

CLASSIC POTATOES AU GRATIN

Spuds are an undeniable comfort, and the pairing of meat and potatoes is probably even more American than apple pie. Scalloped potatoes (au gratin to some) are one of the most agreeable ways of enjoying that comfort, and while several manufacturers produce instant boxed versions, there's nothing like the real thing. This from-scratch recipe, supplied by the company that stands for cheese, may not be particularly quick, but it is otherwise simple to make, and is the perfect potato partner for meat loaf, roast chicken, glazed ham or pork.

6	cups (about 6-8 medium) thinly sliced peeled potatoes
¼	cup PARKAY Margarine
¼	cup flour
1	teaspoon salt
½	teaspoon dry mustard
¼	teaspoon pepper
2½	cups milk
1	8-oz. pkg. (2 cups) 100% Natural KRAFT Shredded Sharp Cheddar Cheese, divided
2	tablespoons chopped onion

CONVENTIONAL

Preheat oven to 350°.

Melt margarine in medium saucepan over medium heat. Blend in flour, salt, mustard and pepper.

Gradually add milk; cook, stirring constantly, until thickened. Add 1½ cups cheese and onion; stir until cheese is melted.

In 2-quart casserole, alternate layers of potatoes and cheese sauce. Bake 1 hour and 15 minutes or until potatoes are tender.

Top with remaining ½ cup cheese; continue baking 5 minutes or until cheese is melted. 6 servings

PREP TIME: 20 minutes   COOKING TIME: 1 hour
                              and 20 minutes

MICROWAVE

In 2-quart casserole, microwave potatoes and ½ cup water on HIGH (100%) 15 to 25 minutes or until tender, stirring every 5 minutes; drain.

In 1-quart bowl, microwave margarine on HIGH (100%) 1 minute or until melted. Blend in flour, salt, mustard, pepper and onion. Gradually add milk.

Microwave on HIGH (100%) 5 to 7 minutes or until thickened, stirring every 2 minutes. Add 1½ cups cheese; stir until melted.

Pour cheese sauce over potatoes; stir. Microwave on HIGH (100%) 4 to 6 minutes or until thoroughly heated, turning dish every 2 minutes.

Top with remaining ½ cup cheese; broil 5 minutes or until cheese is golden brown.

COOKING TIME: 45 minutes

MALLOW-WHIPT SWEET POTATOES

For some Europeans shocked by what Americans eat, ketchup is the symbolic culprit; for others it is the marshmallow—not so much the soft, sweet thing itself as the uses to which we put it. Toasted on a rustic stick, melted in a cup of cocoa or sandwiched with graham crackers and a chocolate bar into the summer camp combo called S'Mores, marshmallows make sense as a kind of multipurpose candy. Why, however, do the crazy Americans put them in salads (*alors!*) or mix them with sweet potatoes and serve them alongside the roasted bird of Thanksgiving, eh? The long history of the national sweet tooth began when the Europeans discovered that some American Indians seasoned virtually everything they ate with maple syrup. Maybe it's something in the water.

Though some people believe marshmallows grow in kitchen cupboards, there is actually a marshmallow plant (*Althaea officinalis*), and the confection was once made from its roots. Now marshmallows are made of corn syrup, cornstarch, gelatin and sugar, and while they are easy to make at home, companies like Kraft and Borden® (whose Campfire® Marshmallows have been manufactured since 1900) do such a good job, there's no need to do it yourself. Of course, marshmallows reached their pinnacle of fame when The Ghostbusters incinerated the Sta-Puft Man at the end of the hit movie. As for the sweet potatoes, there is a long all-American tradition of sweetening them with maple, cider or molasses, one that finds its most modern expression in this sticky classic.

4	cups hot mashed sweet potatoes
¼	cup margarine
¼	cup orange juice
½	teaspoon salt
	KRAFT Miniature Marshmallows

Combine sweet potatoes, margarine, orange juice and salt. Add 1 cup marshmallows; beat until fluffy. Spoon into 1½-quart casserole. Bake at 350°, 20 minutes. Sprinkle with additional marshmallows; broil until lightly browned.

GILDING THE LILY: Coarsely chunked cooked sweet potatoes can be substituted. A touch of cinnamon or a combination of about ¼ teaspoon each cinnamon and nutmeg can be added. The recipe can be doubled or tripled easily, depending on the crowd expected.

CHEESY GARLIC GRITS

Grits (which, by the way, takes the singular verb) is a mystery to most folks who live above the Mason-Dixon line, but in the South this corn product is a starchy, much-loved staple. Cooked into a creamy puddle and buttered to a fare-thee-well, grits goes great with eggs and bacon, ham or sausage. Not to be limited to breakfast time, grits is also an admirable accompaniment to roast pork, beef or roast chicken. One eye-opening answer to the typical pre-supper question, "Rice, potatoes or stuffing, Mom?" is this cheesy, garlic-zapped, atypical formula from the back of the Quaker® box.

3½	cups water
¾	cup QUAKER® Enriched White Hominy Grits
½	teaspoon salt
1	cup (4 oz.) shredded cheddar cheese
2	tablespoons margarine or butter
1	egg, beaten
⅛	teaspoon garlic powder
	Dash of red pepper sauce or ground red pepper (optional)

Heat oven to 350°F. Grease 1½-qt. casserole or baking dish. Prepare grits according to package directions. Stir in remaining ingredients. Continue cooking over low heat until cheese is melted. Pour into prepared casserole; bake 30 minutes. Let stand 5 minutes before serving.

4 to 6 SERVINGS

GILDING THE LILY: One or two cloves of fresh garlic, forced through a press, can be substituted for the garlic powder. Jalapeño jack cheese can be substituted for the cheddar.

PARKS SAVORY SAUSAGE STUFFING

PARKS
Famous Flavor.®

This classic sausage-and-cornbread stuffing recipe appears inside packages of Parks Hot n' Sagey Sausage® only during the Thanksgiving and Christmas holiday seasons. Despite the label's enthusiastic warning ("Very! Hot"), the sausage is only pleasantly *picante*. The stuffing's proportions are perfect, and it is so moist, meaty and authentically Southern that you will want to make it year-round—if you know where to find the recipe.

Parks, an employee-owned meat products company in Baltimore, was founded in 1951 and was the first publicly traded, black-owned American corporation. While its products are available only on the East Coast, Parks has dreams of westward expansion. Until that happens, this simple recipe is good enough to justify making the stuffing with whatever brand of spicy bulk sausage you can find (are you listening, Jimmy Dean?), awaiting the day Parks Hot n' Sagey® shows up in your market. (For 10 to 12 lb. bird)

8	cups bread crumbs (4 soft white + 4 corn bread)*
1	lb. PARKS Hot n' Sagey Sausage®
1	cup chopped onion
1	cup chopped celery
½	cup chopped green pepper
2	teaspoons salt (about)
2	eggs, well beaten
	Liquid from Giblets or Warm Water to moisten

METHOD:

1. Crumble sausage in large skillet and brown lightly, pouring off drippings as it collects, but leaving about 4 tablespoons.
2. Add vegetables and saute slowly until they are clear but not brown.
3. Toss bread with salt—add eggs and mixture of sausage and vegetables.
4. Toss lightly—sprinkle with liquid and mix. You want the stuffing just moist enough to hold a loose ball when you form it with your hand.

More Parks' Sausages, Mom, Please!

*For best results use unsweetened corn bread, no crusts. If corn bread is not available, use soft white bread crumbs entirely.

NOTE: Use PARKS Famous Flavor Sausage® for a milder seasoned dressing.

GILDING THE LILY: Substitute sweet red pepper for the green pepper. For more heat, add 1 fresh jalapeño, minced. Use PARKS milder sausage and replace the green pepper with 1 large apple, cored and chopped. Add ½ cup finely chopped fresh parsley.

FRESH CRANBERRY ORANGE RELISH

Holidays bring the family together, all right, sometimes to celebrate and sometimes to argue about important issues like whether the cranberry sauce should be smooth or chunky. I always loved it smooth (and straight from the can), as did the immediate family, but on certain years we visited relatives who not only put oysters in the turkey stuffing, but served chunky cranberry sauce. The oysters disappeared into the dressing, and if one was careful could be swallowed more or less whole, but the cranberry sauce, with its tangy bits of peel and the occasional whole berry, was just too odd to bear. When we returned home, Mom usually opened a can of *our* kind of cranberry sauce for dinner in the next few days.

Then this cranberry relish—not only chunky but raw—came along, and we loved the orange—a revelation. Now I take cranberries any way I can get them, their brash tartness is welcome to my adult palate, and thanks to the food processor, this fresh relish can be found on my table often. Around Thanksgiving time cranberries are a natural, but for a refreshing change of pace, freeze a bag of berries and try the relish with grilled pork chops, ribs or chicken on a hot July night.

1   package (12 ounces) OCEAN SPRAY® fresh or
        frozen cranberries
1   medium orange
¾-1 cup sugar

Slice unpeeled orange into eighths; remove seeds. Place half the cranberries and half the orange in food processor container. Process until mixture is evenly chopped. Transfer to a bowl. Repeat with remaining cranberries and orange slices. Stir in sugar to desired sweetness. Store in refrigerator or freezer. Makes about 2½ cups. Serve with duck, turkey or chicken, or use the relish to fill pastries and cookies when you bake . . . or to top your favorite cheesecake recipe.

NOTE: May also be prepared in a food grinder.

MOLDED CRANBERRY SALAD

This is a remarkably restrained gelatin-based salad, considering some of the fantastic combinations that turn up on the American table. However you may feel about food that quivers, at holiday time this cranberry classic will convince you it belongs on your plate. It's easy, too.

1	can (8 ounces) crushed pineapple, in own juice
1	package (3 ounces) raspberry flavored gelatin
1	can (16 ounces) OCEAN SPRAY® Whole Berry Cranberry Sauce
¼	cup chopped celery
¼	cup chopped nuts

Drain pineapple, save juice adding enough water to make 1¼ cups liquid. In a saucepan, bring liquid to boil, remove from heat, stir in gelatin until dissolved. Break up cranberry sauce with a fork, stir into gelatin mixture. Cool until mixture begins to thicken, stir in crushed pineapple, celery and nuts. Pour into mold. Chill until set. Makes 8 servings.

EASY MACARONI SALAD

This familiar old recipe probably paved the way for the pasta salad boom of the early Eighties. Many of the country's best and brightest young chefs had eaten plenty of it while growing up, and chilling down every noodle in sight seemed one natural way to marry their raging culinary curiosities with childhood nostalgia. The bad news is, many of the results were, well, bad. The good news is, save for this genuine classic and a handful of successful progeny, pasta salads are no longer a growth industry.

One thoroughly modern foodie confessed to me she so loved her mom's macaroni salad that when she married, she begged for the recipe. Handwritten for her on an index card, it became, over the years, a treasured, much-guarded—and increasingly mayo-spotted—original (she thought) kitchen heirloom—until that fateful day she found it word for word on the Hellmann's® jar, complete down to the indispensable touch of sugar.

According to the Hellmann's® test kitchen, this story is not unique. There are thousands of Americans who can't, or won't, make even so simple a salad without the time-tested back-of-the-jar formula, and when the recipe is even temporarily removed, complaints result.

For others, who like to cook without a net, macaroni salad making is more improvisational, and the salad is slightly different each time it is prepared. There is, however, no need to reinvent the wheel, and adding a little more mayo, and then some more macaroni, and then a little more mayo, etc., may leave you with a very large batch of macaroni salad. By all means add your personal flourishes of jalapeños, pesto, Greek olives, sun-dried tomatoes or sweet pickles, but for ultimate success, experience suggests it is wise to rely on this recipe's classic proportions.

HELLMANN'S REAL MAYONNAISE

1	cup HELLMANN'S® or BEST FOODS® Real Mayonnaise or Light Reduced Calorie Mayonnaise
2	tablespoons vinegar
1	tablespoon prepared mustard
1	teaspoon sugar
1	teaspoon salt
¼	teaspoon pepper
8	ounces MUELLER'S® Elbow Macaroni, cooked and drained
1	cup sliced celery
1	cup chopped green or sweet red pepper
¼	cup chopped onion

In large bowl stir real mayonnaise, vinegar, mustard, sugar, salt and pepper until smooth. Add macaroni, celery, green pepper and onion; toss to coat well. Cover; refrigerate at least 2 hours to blend flavors. Makes 5 cups.

NOTE: If desired, stir in milk for a creamier salad.

CLASSIC POTATO SALAD

No picnic table of my youth was complete without a big, cool crockery bowl of this salad, its top decorated with daisies made of hard-cooked egg segments. The other accompaniments—baked beans, pickled cucumbers, a big plate of sliced beefsteak tomatoes—were almost as essential. There is, after all, a formula for doing these things right.

Back then, of course, the potatoes were thoroughly peeled and cooked to tenderness; today I might prefer to use unpeeled, red-skinned new potatoes, quartered and cooked slightly *al dente*. Either way is good, and either way the salad is the ideal accompaniment to fried chicken, barbecued ribs or grilled burgers.

1	cup HELLMANN'S® or BEST FOODS® Real Mayonnaise
2	tablespoons vinegar
1½	teaspoons salt
1	teaspoon sugar
¼	teaspoon pepper
4	cups cooked, cubed, peeled potatoes (5 to 6 medium)
1	cup sliced celery
½	cup chopped onion
2	hard-cooked eggs, chopped

In large bowl stir together real mayonnaise, vinegar, salt, sugar and pepper until smooth. Add potatoes, celery, onion and eggs; toss to coat well. Cover; refrigerate at least 2 hours to blend flavors. Makes about 5 cups.

GILDING THE LILY: Use sweet red onion or green onion in place of ordinary onion. Use white or red wine vinegar. In season, add ¼ cup chopped fresh dill or basil.

COUNTRY COLE SLAW

The name is from the Dutch word (*koolsla*) for cabbage salad, but slaws can, in fact, be made from things other than cabbage—sauerkraut, carrots or sweet peppers, for example. They can be served hot as well as cold, and the dressing may range from a light vinaigrette to a clingy mayonnaise-based sauce. Some slaws have rather a lot of sugar, and others have none at all. Embellishments might be as obvious as onion and carrot or as unusual as fresh dill and poached shrimp.

Growing up, I remember eating a lettuce slaw, nothing more than chopped iceberg mixed with boiled dressing, always made from my Great-grandmother Walburn's recipe. I haven't had boiled dressing in years (the thought of a flour-thickened sauce on fragile greens is now a little unsettling), but whenever I see the "I Love Lucy" episode where Lucy and Ethel advertise Aunt Martha's Salad Dressing on television, and Lucy enthusiastically swigs the stuff right from the jar, I always remember Great-grandmother's boiled dressing, and I know exactly what Lucy is tasting.

1	cup HELLMANN'S® or BEST FOODS® Real Mayonnaise or Light Reduced Calorie Mayonnaise
3	tablespoons lemon juice
2	tablespoons sugar
1	teaspoon salt
6	cups shredded cabbage
1	cup shredded carrots
½	cup chopped or thinly sliced green pepper

In medium bowl stir real mayonnaise, lemon juice, sugar and salt until smooth. Add cabbage, carrots and green pepper; toss to coat well. Cover; chill. Makes about 6 cups.

GILDING THE LILY: Replace the sweet pepper with diced, unpeeled tart apple. Add coarse-grained mustard to the dressing to taste. Stir in 2 to 3 tablespoons minced fresh dill.

CARROT-PINEAPPLE TOSS

Here is a great example of that particularly American phenomenon—the sweet little salad. Part of a long tradition of tangy, sweetened side dishes (pickled beets, chow-chow, coleslaw, piccalilli, cranberry relish, even ambrosia) reaching back at least to the Pennsylvania Dutch, it is only one example of the sweet-sour craving that finds its fullest expression in the national condiment—ketchup.

One explanation for this yearning is that much of the meat the Colonists had to eat during the country's rough early years had to be salted or smoked to preserve it, and the sweet-and-sour relishes and side dishes provided welcome relief to the palate. That same contrast still works today when this salad is served alongside a good ham, and the satisfying country combination is one I learned to enjoy from the Iowa side of my family. They smoked their own hams on the farm outside Davenport, and served them up often with a salad much like this. It is good, by the way, with many things other than ham.

Carrots, of course, are cheap, readily available, and, goodness knows, good for us. Raisins and pineapple add variety to the version below, and especially now that the food processor is easily coaxed into doing the shredding (use the coarse blade) the salad is quick and keeps its crunchy texture even when a meal lasts for hours.

½	cup SUN-MAID® Seedless Raisins
	Boiling water
1	8¼-ounce can pineapple slices, drained
2	cups shredded carrot
½	cup mayonnaise or salad dressing
1	teaspoon lemon juice (optional)

Place raisins in bowl; cover with boiling water. Let stand 5 minutes; drain well. Cut pineapple into small pieces; mix pineapple with raisins and shredded carrot. Cover and chill. Just before serving, blend in mayonnaise or salad dressing. Sprinkle with lemon juice, if desired. Makes 4 servings.

FIVE-CUP SALAD

If you have been holding your breath, waiting to see if this book contains a recipe combining coconut, marshmallows and fruit, please exhale. Few dishes have undergone changes as dramatic as those that altered the simple, light Southern fruit salad called Ambrosia into a goopy confection more suited to the soda fountain or the dessert course than the buffet table.

The earliest versions of Ambrosia were nothing more than lightly sweetened orange slices sprinkled with shredded coconut. They relied for effect on main ingredients that were novel at that time. As oranges and coconuts became commonplace, the salad was increasingly embellished with grapes, marshmallows, pineapple and creamy mayonnaise or sour cream dressings. Now, *this* is Ambrosia (though if you like it plain and simple, there is, so far, no federal law prohibiting you from doing so), and here is an easy, cup-by-cup approach.

1   cup KRAFT Miniature Marshmallows
1   cup BREAKSTONE'S Sour Cream
1   cup orange sections
1   cup grapes
1   cup flaked coconut

In large bowl, mix together ingredients. Chill.

4 to 6 servings

PREP TIME: 10 minutes plus chilling

VARIATION: Substitute 11-oz. can mandarin orange segments, drained, for orange sections. Add 8-oz. can pineapple chunks, drained.

THREE-BEAN SALAD

It marinates, waiting in the fridge until you're ready; it doesn't wilt on the buffet table; it can be made by merely opening some cans and a bottle and stirring their contents together. Oh, and it tastes great, too, conjuring up images of a steak barbecue on a great rancho somewhere in the easy-living West.

You don't have to serve this salad with steak, but you would be well-advised to try that successful combination, enjoying particularly the taste of steak juices and salad dressing mingled together on the plate (garlic bread is recommended for the mopping up operation). You are also encouraged to improvise freely upon the simple, basic proportions below. For example, for a Southwestern touch, you might like to replace the sweet pickles with roasted red pepper, pickled jalapeño peppers and diced white onion.

1	16 oz. can cut green beans, drained
1	16 oz. can lima beans, drained
1	16 oz. can kidney beans, drained
1	cup chopped tomato
1	cup celery slices
½	cup chopped sweet pickles
	KRAFT French or CATALINA Brand French Dressing

Combine vegetables and enough dressing to moisten; toss lightly. Chill. 10 to 12 servings.

GILDING THE LILY: If you want to spend the kitchen time, frozen green beans and lima beans, lightly cooked, will have better texture than their canned cousins. Garbanzo beans (chick-peas) are a good inclusion. For a less sweet salad, use a bottled Italian-type dressing.

SANDWICHES: HEARTY AND HASTY

Anyone even moderately inclined to collect culinary trivia can tell you that the Earl of Sandwich (the Fourth Earl, Johnny Montagu, to be precise, 1718–1792) was deep into a hot card game when hungry but refusing to leave the gaming table during a lengthy winning streak, he slapped some meat between two pieces of bread and, fortified, continued to woo lady luck. History has honored the earl by naming our favorite casual meal after him, but if you're a real sandwich lover, you may be inclined to feel he had no real idea of what he had started.

The earl's dry and skimpy concoction, eatable, presumably, with only one hand and lacking even mayonnaise (to keep the cards clean), would have the modern American family calling the pizza delivery man in short order. Such survival fare may be acceptable when faced by lonely midnight hungers (or when holding a royal flush), but the Dagwood in all of us demands that a real sandwich be a real handful. Casual as even serious sandwich making is, back-of-the-box gourmets have always known where to turn for a little help.

LIPTON® ONION BURGERS

The same concentrated oniony essence that gives
Lipton® Souperior Meat Loaf (page 34) its flavor
also works in a burger. Especially when turned on
the grill, with all the smoky help charcoal and
mesquite can give, these soup-boosted burgers are a
noticeable improvement over the ordinary sort.
They are also, as any good back-of-the-box recipe
should be, quick and easy to prepare.

1	envelope LIPTON® Onion, Beefy Onion or Beefy Mushroom Recipe Soup Mix
½	cup water
2	pounds ground beef

In large bowl, combine all ingredients. Shape into
8 patties. Grill or broil until done. Makes 8 servings.

MICROWAVE DIRECTIONS: Prepare patties as above.
Place 4 patties in oblong baking dish and heat
uncovered at HIGH (Full Power) 6 minutes, turning
patties once. Repeat with remaining patties. Let
stand covered 5 minutes.

GILDING THE LILY: All of your favorite burger
toppings are fine here, but barely melted goat
cheese or blue cheese are particularly delicious.

CHEESE 'N' WIENER CRESCENTS

At a certain age restless kids need food that is also entertainment. From Mom's point of view that sounds suspiciously like hard work, but it need not be, as this enduring classic shows. Hot dogs always succeed with kids (one young friend of mine even likes them for breakfast), and the simple trick of folding them into a bit of dough instead of an ordinary bun turns a quick supper into a real event. Popping open the dinner roll can is a major part of the show. The baby-sitter can be taught to make these nifty entertainments, and even Dad could probably produce a batch with a little practice. Far from being an outdated oddity from a simpler past, these are still advertised on television—and still enjoyed at home.

8 large wieners
4 slices American cheese, cut into 6 strips each
8-oz. can PILLSBURY Refrigerated Quick Crescent Dinner Rolls

Heat oven to 375°F. Slit wieners to within ½ inch of ends; insert 3 strips cheese in each slit. Separate crescent dough into 8 triangles; wrap dough over wiener keeping cheese up. Place on ungreased cookie sheet, cheese side up. Bake at 375°F. for 12 to 15 minutes or until golden brown. 8 sandwiches.

TIP: To reheat, wrap in foil, heat at 350°F. for 10 to 15 minutes.

FLUFFER-NUTTER

Marshmallow Fluff® goes back to an unrecorded date before World War I when a Boston confectioner whipped up the mixture and sold it door-to-door. After the war, H. Allen Durkee and Fred L. Mower bought the formula and started manufacturing Marshmallow Fluff®, briefly and unwisely calling it "Toot Sweet Marshmallow Fluff." Except for a period when they also produced a hot chocolate mix, the company has specialized in the sugary white stuff ever since.

The peanut butter/marshmallow creme sandwich combination was a New England favorite for years, but reached its present state of national renown only when Durkee-Mower's advertising agency named it in the early Sixties. Here is the official version, from the company's collection of Marshmallow Fluff® recipes, *The Yummy Book*:

> "... spread one piece of bread with Fluff®.
> Then spread another with peanut butter.
> There you have it: a Fluffernutter!"

GILDING THE LILY: Innate sandwich-making instincts tell us to complete the sandwich by pressing the marshmallow and peanut butter-coated sides of the bread together. Whole wheat (or Boston brown) bread adds welcome texture; choosing chunky rather than smooth peanut butter is also a good idea. Sweet jams are redundant, but a thin layer of bittersweet orange marmalade (between the peanut butter and the Marshmallow Fluff®) adds a grown-up touch that may have even the parent/chef enjoying a brown-bag sandwich.

I never took a lunch to school, for when I was old enough to do so, we moved to a house only two blocks from the building, and I went home to eat a hot lunch with the family. This shocking gap in my socialization skills is probably why, even today, I'm: 1) not much of a picnic fan and 2) fascinated by the concept—if not the practice—of brown bagging.

According to my own impromptu survey, none of my lucky friends who took their lunch to school remembers any of the food with much enthusiasm, except for the Fluffernutter. This trusty sandwich is almost more dessert than meal, which is why kids like it, and it is so simple to slap together, it hardly requires directions—or consciousness (which is why Mom and Dad like it). One of its chief virtues is that the parent/chef of the day can have a stack of Fluffernutters ready for the lunch boxes without actually waking up. After school, of course, kids can—and will—make their own.

FROSTED SANDWICH LOAF

Kraft was a major television advertiser for years, first entering the market in 1947 with "Kraft Television Theater." For several generations, their 90-second-long "omnibus" commercials, showing a full-course meal, demonstrated by anonymous hands and narrated by the mellow voice of Ed Herlihy, were windows into a colorful world of easy food.

As a child I relished these mouth-watering commercials in all their stylish glory, and I'm convinced that those intense close-ups of food preparations are one of the main reasons I'm in the cooking business today. (Apparently the rest of America agreed, because Kraft sales boomed.)

One fondly remembered assembly is this complicated sandwich loaf, a classic originally from the "elegant 1920s," according to one Kraft cookbook. The recipe gives no directions for slicing the assembled loaf, nor for managing to pick up and eat the resulting cream cheese-coated sandwiches—technical omissions which with youthful energy and enthusiasm I blithely overlooked, easy to do since I never attempted it. Nowadays I'm suspicious of foods that look too pretty to eat, but I'm still fascinated by the sandwich loaf and hope someday someone will make one for me.

6	hard-cooked eggs, finely chopped
1	teaspoon prepared mustard
¼	teaspoon salt
	Dash of pepper
	Mayonnaise

* * *

2	cups finely chopped ham
¼	cup finely chopped sweet pickle
	Mayonnaise

* * *

3	8-oz pkgs. PHILADELPHIA BRAND Cream Cheese
¼	cup finely chopped watercress
	Dash of salt and pepper

* * *

1	unsliced sandwich loaf, 16 inches long
	Soft margarine
¼	cup milk

Combine eggs, mustard, seasonings and enough mayonnaise to moisten; mix lightly.

Combine meat, pickle and enough mayonnaise to moisten; mix lightly.

Combine ½ package softened cream cheese, watercress and seasonings, mixing well until blended.

Trim crust from bread; cut into four lengthwise slices. Spread bread slices with margarine. Spread one bread slice with egg salad, a second slice with ham salad, and a third slice with cream cheese mixture. Stack layers; cover with fourth bread slice. Combine remaining cream cheese and milk, mixing until well blended. Frost sandwich loaf; chill thoroughly.

VARIATIONS: Thinly sliced tomatoes or cucumbers or cheese slices may be substituted for either of the salad fillings.

Decorate the loaf with colorful garnishes such as sliced ripe or stuffed olives, radish roses, carrot curls or watercress.

BREAKFAST AND BRUNCH: PANCAKES, WAFFLES, QUICK BREADS AND MUFFINS

Good morning! Need help getting breakfast on the table? Weekdays, forget it—food is fuel, and the simpler and speedier the better. Weekends, though, a lazy breakfast or self-indulgent brunch is one of the last great luxuries, and those who have bolted the first meal of the day Monday through Friday deserve something a little special come Saturday. Achieving this delightful repast without squandering your day off as a short-order cook is easier than you may think.

Compared to a bagel on the train, a cup of yogurt at your desk, the oatmeal the kids didn't finish or one of those steamed breakfast hockey pucks from the folks with the golden arches, even simple bacon and eggs with a little defrosted orange juice sipped at leisure can seem like a banquet. These easy indulgences plus the Sunday funnies do very nicely indeed, but when you want to go above and beyond even ordinary weekend excess, breakfast and brunch can always get a boost from the following back-of-the-box recipes. Pancakes, waffles, muffins and quick breads—even fresh corn bread —are the kind of seductive but easy treats that can make a Sunday truly special. More syrup, please.

GOOD MORNING PUMPKIN PANCAKES

In large mixer bowl, combine biscuit mix, sugar, cinnamon, and allspice. Add evaporated milk, pumpkin, oil, eggs, and vanilla; beat until smooth. Pour ¼ to ½ cup batter (depending on size of pancake desired) onto heated and lightly greased griddle. Cook until top surface is bubbly and edges are dry. Turn, cook until golden. Keep pancakes warm. Serve with syrup or honey. (Makes about 16 pancakes.)

GILDING THE LILY: Add about ½ cup chopped pecans to the batter. Top the pancakes with a mixture of softened butter and orange marmalade.

Delicious and handsomely colored, these pumpkin flapjacks are not just for holiday time. Year-round (as long as that essential canned pumpkin is in the cupboard), teamed with butter, maple syrup or honey, and ham or bacon, they'll have everyone wide awake and ready for seconds.

2	cups biscuit mix
2	tablespoons packed light brown sugar
2	teaspoons ground cinnamon
1½	cups (12-ounce can) *undiluted* CARNATION® Evaporated Milk
1	teaspoon ground allspice
½	cup LIBBY'S® Solid Pack Pumpkin
2	tablespoons vegetable oil
2	eggs
1	teaspoon vanilla extract

CHOCOLATE PECAN WAFFLES WITH FRUIT TOPPING

The suggested warm fruit toppings make these waffles seriously celebratory. More sedate morning feeders will find butter and maple syrup closer to their liking.

½ cup HERSHEY®'S Cocoa
¼ cup butter or margarine, melted
¾ cup sugar
2 eggs
2 teaspoons vanilla extract
1 cup all-purpose flour
½ teaspoon baking soda
½ teaspoon salt
½ cup buttermilk or sour milk*
½ cup chopped pecans (optional)
   Apple-Cinnamon Topping (recipe follows)
   Peach-Nutmeg Topping (recipe follows)

In small mixer bowl blend cocoa and melted butter until smooth; stir in sugar. Add eggs and vanilla; beat well. Combine flour, baking soda and salt; add alternately with buttermilk to cocoa mixture. Stir in pecans, if desired. Bake in waffle iron on low setting according to manufacturer's directions. Carefully remove waffle from iron. Serve warm with fruit topping of your choice. About ten 4-inch waffles.

*To sour milk: Use 1½ teaspoons vinegar plus milk to equal ½ cup.

Apple-Cinnamon Topping—In small saucepan heat 1 can (21-ounces) apple pie filling, 1 tablespoon butter and ⅛ teaspoon ground cinnamon until warm.

Peach-Nutmeg Topping—In small saucepan heat 1 can (21-ounces) peach pie filling and ⅛ teaspoon ground nutmeg until warm.

GILDING THE LILY: Turn these into dessert waffles by topping them with a scoop of strawberry ice cream and a drizzle of warm Hot Fudge Sauce (page 81).

OUR BEST
BRAN MUFFINS

Here, in the midst of a chapter dedicated to unbridled hedonism, is a small, sane voice of nutritional restraint—undone only slightly by the fact that muffins, even healthy ones, are always a treat. Perhaps it's the shape.

1¼	cups all-purpose flour
1	tablespoon baking powder
½	teaspoon salt
½	cup sugar
1½	cups KELLOGG'S® ALL-BRAN® cereal
1¼	cups milk
1	egg
¼	cup vegetable oil

1. Stir together flour, baking powder, salt and sugar; set aside.

2. Measure KELLOGG'S® ALL-BRAN® cereal and milk into large bowl. Stir to combine. Let stand 5 minutes. Add egg and oil; beat well.

3. Add flour mixture, stirring only until combined. Portion batter evenly into 12 greased 2½-inch muffin-pan cups.

4. Bake in 400°F oven for 18 to 20 minutes.

YIELD: 12 muffins

FOR MUFFINS WITH REDUCED CALORIES, FAT, SODIUM, AND SUGAR: Use ¼ teaspoon salt, 2 tablespoons sugar and 2 tablespoons vegetable oil. Use skim milk in place of whole milk.

GILDING THE LILY: Add ¾ cup raisins to the batter. Leftover muffins can be reheated in the microwave.

CHIQUITA® BANANA PANCAKES WITH BANANA HONEY TOPPING

What is it about kids and bananas? It beats me, since I grew up hating this most popular fruit in America (sorry, apple fans). In fact, though they sat in a basket on top of our refrigerator, slowly turning black, I don't remember anyone in the family ever actually eating a banana. Perhaps they had some special use in the compost heap.

Well, I turned out tall, strong and healthy without ever eating bananas, leading me to the personal conclusion that they aren't all that nutritionally essential. That argument won't hold water with the rest of the country's kids, who apparently believe in the modern axiom "a banana a day, etc., etc." Among the most agreeable ways of getting the daily doses are these flapjacks, from (who else?) that legendary spokesbanana, Chiquita®. They're easy to make, and judging from the happy noises at a recent breakfast table, banana lovers of all ages find them delicious.

Make pancake mix according to the directions on the package. To each cup of batter add ½ cup of diced or sliced CHIQUITA® Brand Bananas. Cook, following the directions on the package mix package, until golden. Serve with the following topping:

BANANA HONEY TOPPING

2   ripe CHIQUITA® Brand Bananas
2-4 tablespoons honey, to taste
2   tablespoons softened butter or margarine

Peel the bananas. In a bowl, mash them together with the honey and butter.

EASY CORN BREAD

Corn, a native crop of the Western Hemisphere, was a staple long before the pilgrims arrived. In fact, with help from the Indians, corn kept the colonists alive that first harsh winter and for years to follow. The Indians ground the dried corn to a meal and baked it in the fire, producing a rough bread, or pone. Modern corn bread is merely a lighter, more tender version of this early staple.

Many Southerners prefer white corn meal (there's no flavor difference), and the bread is sweetened subtly, if at all. Northerners expect a yellow corn bread with a sweeter taste. Fortunately, like many such regional food disagreements, the corn bread controversy is rooted in a common love for the dish in question, and there is no record of blows being exchanged. Northerners and Southerners alike will recognize this recipe (and the great berry muffin variation) for its classic simplicity and perfect proportions.

1¼	cups all-purpose flour
¾	cup QUAKER® or AUNT JEMIMA® Enriched Corn Meal
¼	cup sugar
2	teaspoons baking powder
½	teaspoon salt (optional)
1	cup skim milk
¼	cup vegetable oil
2	egg whites or 1 egg, beaten

Heat oven to 400°F. Grease 8 or 9-inch baking pan. Combine dry ingredients. Stir in milk, oil and egg, mixing just until dry ingredients are moistened. Pour batter into prepared pan. Bake 20 to 25 minutes or until light golden brown and wooden pick inserted near center comes out clean. Serve warm. 9 SERVINGS

VARIATION: Corn Berry Muffins. Grease bottoms only of 12 medium muffin cups or line with paper baking cups. Add one cup fresh or frozen blueberries, partially thawed, to batter. Fill prepared muffin cups ¾ full. Bake 20 to 25 minutes or until light golden brown. 1 DOZEN

GILDING THE LILY: Buttermilk can be substituted for the skim milk. Melted butter can be substituted for the oil. Fresh or unsweetened frozen raspberries can be substituted for the blueberries in the muffins.

CRANBERRY NUT BREAD

A slice of this sweet and tangy bread is delicious with a schmear of cream cheese. The loaf also makes great holiday giving.

2   cups all-purpose flour
1   cup sugar
1½   teaspoons baking powder
1   teaspoon salt
½   teaspoon baking soda
¾   cup orange juice
1   tablespoon grated orange peel
2   tablespoons shortening
1   egg, well beaten
1½   cups OCEAN SPRAY® fresh or frozen cranberries,
        coarsely chopped
½   cup chopped nuts

Preheat oven to 350°F. In a bowl, mix together flour, sugar, baking powder, salt and baking soda. Stir in orange juice, orange peel, shortening and egg. Mix until well blended. Stir in cranberries and nuts. Turn into a 9″ × 5″ loaf pan, greased on bottom only. Bake for 55 minutes or until toothpick inserted in center comes out clean. Cool on a rack 15 minutes; remove from pan. Makes 1 loaf.

CHOCOLATE: SWEET SEDUCTION

What can be said about chocolate that you haven't already confided to your diary, your therapist or your tailor? If you feel haunted, obsessed by, perhaps a trifle addicted to the rich sweet stuff, take consolation in the fact that you're not alone. Each and every American will consume an average of 10 pounds or so of chocolate this year (not at one sitting of course, although it seems like that sometimes), and though tastes run the gamut from cheap little bars of doubtful quality to hunks of the best imported examples of European chocolate-making skills, our craving remains the same.

Produced, through a lengthy and complicated process, from the bitter, fatty seed pods of a tropical evergreen tree, chocolate contains some 370 separate volatile chemical compounds—any one of which may well account for the subtle magic that has captivated man for centuries. Though the Aztecs first made use of chocolate (drinking it hot, unsweetened and spiked with chiles), it was the Spanish who first added sugar, setting chocolate on the path to the seductive sweet we yearn for today. At first they tried to keep it a secret, but chocolate was simply too good to suppress, and soon after there were American colonies, there were Americans manufacturing chocolate.

The news for back-of-the-box gourmets is good. Though chocolate—as you already know—is wonderful eaten out of hand, it's also a basic cooking ingredient, and American companies have produced thousands of tantalizing recipes for turning tempting chocolate into tempting desserts. Herewith some favorites.

NO-BAKE CHOCOLATE CHEESECAKE

To the ears of many cooks, the phrase "no-bake" is music, signaling that the kitchen time, oven heat and other nasty complications have been removed from an otherwise tricky recipe by some kindly soul, leaving only delicious results behind. Frequently, however, no-bake recipes are rather half-baked, and not even worth the little time they take to prepare. This cheesecake is a notable exception. Since it needs some refrigerated chilling time, it can't be called spontaneous, but otherwise it is the answer to a no-bake chocolate prayer.

1½ cups HERSHEY®'S Semi-Sweet Chocolate Chips
1   package (8 ounces) cream cheese, softened
1   package (3 ounces) cream cheese, softened
½   cup sugar
¼   cup butter or margarine, softened
2   cups frozen non-dairy whipped topping, thawed
8-inch (6 ounces) packaged graham cracker
      crumb crust

In small microwave-safe bowl place chocolate chips. Microwave at HIGH (100%) 1 to 1½ minutes or until chips are melted and mixture is smooth when stirred. Set aside to cool. In large mixer bowl beat cream cheese, sugar and butter until smooth. On low speed blend in melted chocolate. Fold in whipped topping until blended; spoon cheese mixture into crust. Cover; chill until firm. Garnish as desired. About 8 servings.

GILDING THE LILY: Garnish each slice of cheesecake with a dollop of whipped cream (or whipped topping) and a sprinkle of chocolate chips.

ORIGINAL CHOCOLATE MAYONNAISE CAKE

1	teaspoon baking soda
1	cup boiling water
1	cup coarsely chopped dates
1	cup coarsely chopped walnuts
1	cup sugar
1	cup real mayonnaise
6	tablespoons grated unsweetened chocolate
1	teaspoon vanilla
2	cups unsifted cake flour

Grease and flour 9 × 9 × 2-inch baking pan. In small bowl stir baking soda and boiling water until dissolved. Stir in dates and nuts. In large bowl with mixer at low speed beat sugar and real mayonnaise until well blended. Add chocolate and vanilla; beat until blended. Add date mixture; beat until well mixed. Gradually beat in flour until smooth. Turn into prepared pan. Bake in 350°F. oven 45 to 50 minutes or until cake tester inserted in center comes out clean. Cool in pan. Frost if desired. Makes 9 servings.

GILDING THE LILY: Frosting, in this case, may well be gilding the lily, and the moist, dense cake is delicious with nothing more than a simple dusting of powdered sugar and, occasionally, a dollop of unsweetened real whipped cream. For those who believe the reason for eating cake *is* frosting, however, I suggest the No-Cook Fudge Frosting on page 83.

Mr. Hellmann's New York delicatessen became, circa 1912, as famous for the house mayonnaise as for the sandwiches on which it was spread. Because of popular demand, quarts of the unctuous stuff were made available to go, freeing cooks from the rather iffy process of whisking up their own at home. Soon the mayonnaise *was* the business, and, in 1937, one sales distributor's wife created a cake using mayonnaise as a main ingredient.

It's not as strange as it sounds. The eggs and oil provide moistness and the lemon juice adds a distinctive bit of acid that makes the cake splendidly tender without actually *tasting* like mayonnaise. Mrs. Paul Price's original mayonnaise cake was moist, brownie-like, date- and walnut-studded. Though there is a now plainer version (minus fruit and nuts) in circulation, this original is well worth the brief kitchen time it takes to create.

HOT FUDGE SAUCE

Fast, good and chocolate, three of my favorite words, all accurately describe this sauce. At the soda fountain in my hometown Rexall drug store (eliminated years ago during a traumatic remodeling), where the limeade was made from just-squeezed limes, the Spanish peanuts rained down with generous abandon and the cherry Cokes and Green Rivers flowed like, well, like rivers, I don't think the hot fudge sauce was homemade, but if it had been, it would have been just like this thick, dark expression of chocolate intensity. Great on a banana split, a spoon, a finger . . .

¾   cup sugar
½   cup HERSHEY₍®₎'S Cocoa
½   cup plus 2 tablespoons (5-ounce can)
        evaporated milk
⅓   cup light corn syrup
⅓   cup butter or margarine
1   teaspoon vanilla extract

In medium saucepan combine sugar and cocoa; blend in evaporated milk and corn syrup. Cook over medium heat, stirring constantly, until mixture boils; boil and stir 1 minute. Remove from heat; stir in butter and vanilla. Serve warm. About 1¾ cups sauce.

GILDING THE LILY: Stir 2 or 3 tablespoons of appropriate, chocolate-compatible liqueur, such as Grand Marnier, dark rum, or Kahlúa, into the finished sauce.

SIGNATURE BROWNIES

Sadly, the story of the creation of the brownie is unknown. If ever the originator of something good to eat deserved honor, it's that first brownie baker, whoever she or he may have been. Commonly credited to an anonymous forgetful cook who left the leavening out of a chocolate cake, brownies are such a direct, simple way to enjoy chocolate that it's hard to imagine they weren't concocted on purpose by someone who had a very definite chocolate-loving goal in mind. One of the earliest mentions of the brownie in print came in the 1897 *Sears Roebuck and Co. Catalog,* which means a Centennial celebration is coming up. On this auspicious near-anniversary, as we raise a toast (or at least a brownie) to that unknown genius, let us also agree never again to dismiss the brownie as something that happened by accident.

Connoisseurs may quibble over cake-like versus fudgy, over whether frosting and nuts belong in or out, over who gets to lick the spoon, but all agree that timely gratification of the chocolate craving remains the main reason for the brownie's popularity.

1	package (15 ounces) golden sugar cookie mix
½	cup HERSHEY®'S Cocoa
½	cup HERSHEY®'S Syrup
¼	cup butter or margarine, melted
1	egg
½	cup coarsely chopped nuts
	No-Cook Fudge Frosting (recipe follows)

Heat oven to 350°. Grease 8- or 9-inch square baking pan. In medium bowl combine cookie mix (and enclosed flavor packet) and cocoa. Stir in syrup, butter and egg, blending well. Stir in nuts. Spread into prepared pan. Bake 25 to 30 minutes or until wooden pick inserted in center comes out clean. Cool completely. Frost with No-Cook Fudge Frosting. Cut into bars. About 20 brownies.

No-Cook Fudge Frosting—In small bowl combine 2 cups confectioners' sugar, ½ cup HERSHEY®'S Syrup, ¼ cup HERSHEY®'S Cocoa, ¼ cup melted butter or margarine and ½ teaspoon vanilla extract; blend well. Use immediately.

TUNNEL OF FUDGE CAKE

Submitted by Ella Helfrich of Houston, Texas, the Tunnel of Fudge Cake won second prize (and $5,000) in the 1966 Pillsbury Bake-Off®. It also boosted the sales of a type of cake pan new to most American cooks—the Bundt. (Pillsbury alone fielded 200,000 requests for the then-unfamiliar pan.) Moist, walnut-studded and chocolate, with a rich center of gooey fudge, the cake has been a favorite for years. In a reversal of the usual back-of-the-box trend, the cake has recently been modified by a Pillsbury home economist to replace the increasingly hard-to-find boxed frosting mix (the source of the "tunnel") with a scratch equivalent.

CAKE

1¾   cups margarine or butter, softened
1¾   cups granulated sugar
6   eggs
2   cups powdered sugar
2¼   cups Pillsbury's BEST® All Purpose Flour
¾   cup cocoa
2   cups chopped walnuts*

GLAZE

¾   cup powdered sugar
¼   cup cocoa
1½-2 tablespoons milk

Heat oven to 350°F. Grease and flour 12-cup fluted tube pan or 10-inch angel food tube pan. In large bowl, beat margarine and granulated sugar until light and fluffy. Add eggs, one at a time, beating well after each addition. Gradually add powdered sugar; blend well. By hand, stir in remaining cake ingredients until well blended. Spoon batter into prepared pan; spread evenly. Bake at 350°F. for 58 to 62 minutes.** Cool upright in pan on cooling rack 1 hour; invert onto serving plate. Cool completely.

In small bowl, combine glaze ingredients until well blended. Spoon over top of cake, allowing some to run down sides. Store tightly covered. 16 servings.

TIPS: *Nuts are essential for the success of the recipe.

**Since this cake has a soft tunnel of fudge, ordinary doneness test cannot be used. Accurate oven temperature and bake time are critical.

HIGH ALTITUDE—Above 3500 feet: Increase flour to 2¼ cups plus 3 tablespoons.

FAMOUS CHOCOLATE REFRIGERATOR ROLL

This simple little sweet from the Nabisco® test kitchens, really nothing more than chocolate cookies and whipped cream, boasts legions of loyal fans. When the cookies and cream are alternately layered in a sideways stack, or roll, and chilled for a time, the cookies absorb some of the whipped cream and become moist and cake-like. Sliced on the bias, the "roll" reveals a decoratively zebra-striped oval. A slice (or two or three) can be arranged on a plate and garnished with fresh strawberries, raspberries or bananas and additional whipped cream, producing a socially acceptable company dessert version of everyone's favorite consolation snack—cookies and milk. The downside to all this is that Famous Chocolate Wafers are not available in all areas, a state of affairs that frankly adds to the dessert's mystique and frequently leads those more fortunate to ship regular care packages to their underprivileged friends in other parts of the country.

1	cup heavy cream
2	tablespoons granulated sugar
½	teaspoon vanilla extract
20	FAMOUS Chocolate Wafers
	Red candied cherries, optional

Whip cream with sugar and vanilla until stiff. Spread wafers with part of cream. Put together in stacks of 4 or 5. Chill 15 minutes. Stand stacks on edge on plate to make one long roll. Frost outside of roll with remaining cream. Refrigerate at least three hours. Garnish with red candied cherries, if desired. Cut diagonally at a 45° angle. Makes 8 (about ¾-inch) slices.

Roll may be frozen, if desired. Remove from freezer to refrigerator about one hour before serving.

BLENDER MINT MOUSSE

1   10-oz. pkg. NESTLÉ® TOLL HOUSE®
      Mint-Chocolate Morsels
2   eggs
1   cup scalded milk
      Whipped Cream (optional)

Corporate test kitchens are always quick to adapt their back-of-the-box classics to current technology, and since the food processor and the microwave oven now dominate the way we want to cook, convenience recipes reflect that trend. Not that long ago, however, there was a blender-obsessed phase of American cookery, whereby that handy kitchen counter gadget was expected to do everything except the dishes. This mint-chocolate mousse from Nestlé® stubbornly resists updating and still works best in the blender for which it was originally developed. The result (particularly when contrasted with the multi-step, two- or three-bowl, genuine French original) is so simple and so good, its rediscovery could lead to a revival of blender cuisine.

In blender container, combine NESTLÉ® TOLL HOUSE® mint-chocolate morsels, eggs and scalded milk. Cover; blend on high speed 2–3 minutes. Pour into individual serving dishes. Garnish with unsweetened whip cream, if desired.

Makes: 4 servings

GILDING THE LILY: The recipe neglects to mention chilling the mousses for an hour or two, or until set. Non-mint morsels can be substituted, and if you do so, a tablespoon or two of Grand Marnier or other chocolate-compatible liqueur can be added.

NEVER-FAIL FUDGE

The existence of never-fail fudge unfortunately verifies the existence of the other kind. If you've ever had a batch turn on you, you'll understand the validity of that glum expression of failure, "Oh, fudge!" Making fudge disaster-proof seems to have occupied test kitchens for years—no mean accomplishment, since chocolate in general and the molten sugar syrup of classic fudge-making in specific are loaded with things that can go wrong. One of the best of the foolproof fudges is the following one, which uses Marshmallow Fluff®.

The recipe is said to have been Mamie Eisenhower's, with all the sweet Fifties charm that connotes, and it was originally published to great acclaim in co-op ads with Nestlé®. Nowadays the brand of chocolate chips is not specified, but otherwise the recipe remains unchanged, and it is, well, a sure thing.

2½ c. sugar
½   stick butter or margarine
1   small can evaporated milk (5-oz.)
1   7½-oz. jar MARSHMALLOW FLUFF® (2 c.)
¾   tsp. salt
¾   tsp. vanilla extract
1   12-oz. package semisweet-chocolate pieces
½   c. chopped walnuts

Grease a 9-inch square baking pan; set aside. In large saucepan combine first 5 ingredients. Stir over low heat until blended. Bring to a full-rolling boil being careful not to mistake escaping air bubbles for boiling. Boil slowly, stirring constantly, 5 minutes, (soft ball stage). Remove from heat, stir in vanilla and chocolate until chocolate is melted. Add nuts. Turn into greased pan and cool. Makes 2½ pounds.

MICROWAVE FUDGE INSTRUCTIONS

1. Combine first 5 ingredients in a 4 qt. microwave safe bowl. Microwave at medium high for 2½ minutes; remove and stir until blended.

2. Microwave at medium high for 5 minutes; remove and stir until smooth.

3. Repeat step 2.

4. Microwave at medium high for 6 minutes; remove and stir in chocolate, vanilla and nuts for 5 minutes until thick. Turn into buttered 9 × 9 in. pan and cool.

IMPORTANT, Instructions are for a *600 watt microwave oven.* For a different size oven, adjust cooking accordingly.

CAKES: HIGH, LIGHT AND HANDSOME

Some otherwise perfectly good cooks can't make cakes from scratch. Haunted by so many homemade failures, we can perhaps be forgiven when we resort to mixes. If only cakes were as simple as cookies! If only they weren't such *visible* examples of our ineptitude—tilting at odd angles, stapled together under all that frosting with invisible but potentially lethal toothpicks, remaining behind on the bake sale table while all the mix cakes are snatched up by those for whom beauty is only icing deep.

The test kitchens of corporate America know well the ways a cake can go wrong and have dedicated thousands of hours and unlimited ingenuity to foolproofing the process. From the backs of many boxes come high, wide, handsome and genuinely homemade-tasting cakes that have been developed to make the clumsiest baker feel proud of the results. It should be added that while not all of these recipes are exactly speedy (for that, a mix still can't be beat) they are either models of simplicity or endearingly gimmicky—as well as surprisingly delicious.

GERMAN'S® SWEET CHOCOLATE CAKE

If you've ever wondered about the name and origins of this classic American cake, you're not alone. Though I chose it year after year for my birthday celebration, I never knew the story, and until work on this collection of back-of-the-box recipes came along, I never had the chance to track it down. For those impressed by the details of the Toll House® tale (page 116), this one remains intriguingly similar, even though there is no single creator to credit.

One of the first companies to manufacture chocolate in America was financed by James Baker in 1765. A descendant, Walter Baker, had an English employee named Samuel German, who, around 1850, developed the formula for a so-called sweet (some experts have actually called it bittersweet) chocolate. Added to the Baker's® line, the product sold steadily—if unremarkably—for years.

In 1957, a cake recipe that used German's® Sweet Chocolate was submitted by a reader and appeared in a Dallas newspaper. The recipe, which featured a coconut-pecan frosting sandwiched between 3 chocolate cake layers, caused a boom in regional chocolate sales so dramatic it drew the attention of a General Foods district manager. He then located the recipe and sent it to the test kitchens. It was perfected—and named—and the company's publicity machinery went into full gear, submitting the recipe, along with photos and supporting material, to food editors around the country. The same enthusiasm that Texans felt for the cake was soon evident everywhere, and in only a short time German's® Sweet Chocolate Cake was an American classic.

Though the brouhaha was new, the cake, apparently, was not. One reader, delighted at seeing the recipe in print again, wrote to say it almost duplicated a pre-Depression era formula she had been given by her mother-in-law. The Texas touches of buttermilk, coconut and pecans hint that if it wasn't developed in the Lone Star State, it was at least destined to begin its rise to prominence there; the rest is speculation. As with many of the best of the back-of-the-box recipes, even though it existed before it went onto the package, the cake never achieved true fame until it became associated with a product and was promoted with all the energy a dedicated American corporation can muster.

1 package (4 oz.) BAKER'S® GERMAN'S® Sweet Chocolate
½ cup boiling water
2¼ cups cake flour*
1 teaspoon baking soda
½ teaspoon salt
1 cup butter or margarine
2 cups sugar
4 egg yolks
1 teaspoon vanilla
1 cup buttermilk
4 egg whites
  Coconut-Pecan Filling and Frosting

Melt chocolate in boiling water; cool. Mix flour with soda and salt; set aside. Cream butter and sugar in large bowl until light and fluffy. Add egg yolks, one at a time, beating after each addition. Blend in vanilla and melted chocolate. Add flour mixture, alternately with the buttermilk, beating after each addition until smooth.

Beat egg whites until they form stiff peaks; fold into batter. Pour batter into three 9-inch layer pans which have been lined on bottoms with waxed paper. Bake at 350° for 30 minutes or until cake springs back when lightly pressed in center.

Remove from oven; immediately run spatula around between cake and sides of pans. Cool cake in pans 15 minutes; then remove and cool on rack.

Spread Coconut-Pecan Filling and Frosting between layers and over top of cake.

NOTE: This delicate cake will have a flat slightly sugary top crust which tends to crack.

*Or use 2 cups all-purpose flour

COCONUT-PECAN FILLING AND FROSTING

1½ cups (12 fl. oz. can) evaporated milk
1½ cups sugar
4 egg yolks, slightly beaten
¾ cup butter or margarine
1½ teaspoons vanilla
2 cups BAKER'S® ANGEL FLAKE® Coconut
1½ cups chopped pecans

Combine milk, sugar, egg yolks, butter and vanilla in saucepan. Cook and stir over medium heat until mixture thickens and is golden brown, about 12 minutes. Remove from heat. Add coconut and pecans. Beat until cool and of spreading consistency. Makes about 4¼ cups, or enough to frost tops of two 13 × 9-inch cakes, or fill and frost 3-layer cake.

ALTERNATE BAKING PANS

Two 8-inch square pans for 45 to 50 minutes
Two 9-inch square pans for 40 to 45 minutes
One 13 × 9-inch pan for 55 minutes

In high altitude areas, do not separate eggs; increase flour to 2¾ cups and salt to 1 teaspoon; reduce butter to ¾ cup and sugar to 1½ cups (at 3000 to 5000 ft., use 1¾ c.); bake at 375°.

MILKY WAY® BAR SWIRL CAKE

The Milky Way® Bar, introduced around 1923, was inspired by the flavors of a chocolate malted. This handsome cake shares that quality and is generously swirled within as well as glazed on top with malty melted candy bar.

2   MILKY WAY® Bars (2.23 oz. ea.), sliced
1   cup plus 2 tablespoons water
1   pkg. (18½ oz.) pudding-in-the-mix yellow cake mix
⅓   cup vegetable oil
3   eggs, at room temperature
2   tablespoons all-purpose flour
    MILKY WAY® Bar Glaze*

Stir 2 MILKY WAY® Bars and 2 tablespoons water in a medium saucepan over low heat until smooth; let cool slightly. Meanwhile generously grease and flour 12-cup Bundt-type pan. Mix the cake mix, 1 cup water, oil and eggs in a large bowl and with an electric mixer beat at low speed until combined.

Beat 2 minutes at high speed. Blend ⅔ cup batter and the flour into the MILKY WAY® Bar mixture. Pour the remaining plain batter into prepared pan. **Spoon** the MILKY WAY® Bar onto the batter; do not allow it to touch the sides of the pan. Run a knife through the batters to swirl. **Bake at 350°F.** for 40 minutes or until cake tests done. **Cool** cake in pan on cooling rack for 25 minutes. Remove from pan and cool completely. Sprinkle cake, if desired, with confectioners' sugar, then drizzle with **Glaze.** Makes about 12 servings.

*MILKY WAY® Bar Glaze: Stir 2 MILKY WAY® Bars, sliced; 2 tablespoons butter and 2 teaspoons water in a small saucepan over low heat until smooth. Let cool slightly to reach a glaze consistency.

CLASSIC TOMATO SOUP CAKE

Sometimes called Tomato Cake or Mystery Cake, this otherwise fairly traditional spice cake gains moisture, a touch of flavor and an attractive reddish-orange color from the can of tomato soup in the batter. When you think about it, it's no odder than using mayonnaise or salad dressing, now is it?

2	cups all-purpose flour
1⅓	cups sugar
4	teaspoons baking powder
1	teaspoon baking soda
1½	teaspoons ground allspice
1	teaspoon ground cinnamon
½	teaspoon ground cloves
1	can (10¾ ounces) CAMPBELL'S® Condensed Tomato Soup
½	cup shortening
2	eggs
¼	cup water

1. Preheat oven to 350°F. Grease and flour two 8-inch round cake pans.

2. In large bowl, combine all ingredients. With mixer at low speed, beat until well mixed, constantly scraping bowl with rubber spatula. At high speed, beat 4 minutes, occasionally scraping bowl. Pour into prepared pans.

3. Bake 35 to 40 minutes or until toothpick inserted in center comes out clean. Cool in pans on wire racks 10 minutes. Remove from pans; cool completely. Frost with your favorite cream cheese frosting if desired. Makes 12 servings.

GILDING THE LILY: Add 1 cup raisins and/or 1 cup walnuts to the batter. Frost with Vanilla "Philly" Frosting (page 97).

EASY CARROT CAKE

Here's another cake that augments a standard mix with a distinctive ingredient—carrots, paired with the traditional cream cheese frosting. Kraft Miracle Whip Salad Dressing, introduced in 1933 as a blend of mayonnaise and "old-fashioned boiled dressing," helps make the cake rich, moist and tender.

1	two-layer yellow cake mix
1¼	cups MIRACLE WHIP Salad Dressing
4	eggs
¼	cup cold water
2	teaspoons cinnamon
2	cups finely shredded carrots
½	cup chopped walnuts

Combine cake mix, salad dressing, eggs, water and cinnamon, mixing at medium speed with electric mixer until well blended. Stir in carrots and walnuts.

Pour into greased 13 × 9-inch baking pan.

Bake 350°, 30 to 35 minutes or until wooden pick inserted in center comes out clean. Cool; frost with:

VANILLA "PHILLY" FROSTING

1   8-oz. pkg. PHILADELPHIA BRAND Cream Cheese, softened
1   tablespoon vanilla
3-3½ cups sifted powdered sugar

In small, high-sided mixing bowl, use electric mixer to beat cream cheese and vanilla, mixing until well blended.

Gradually add sugar, beating until light and fluffy. 10 to 12 servings

PREP TIME: 25 minutes   COOKING TIME: 35 minutes plus cooling

GILDING THE LILY: For an added fillip, ½ cup raisins can be added along with the carrots and walnuts. The batter can also be baked as cupcakes. A squeeze of fresh lemon juice can be added to the frosting, along with or in place of the vanilla.

HOLLYWOOD CHEESECAKE

Despite its glamorous West Coast name, this cheesecake is pure middle America. In one city of my youth there was a tiny Italian restaurant famed for its cheesecake. If you knew someone who knew someone, you might be lucky enough to get a contraband copy of the recipe, but you were sworn not to pass it on, not to reveal from whom you received it and never upon penalty of death to tell anyone connected with the restaurant that one of the secrets of its success was slowly leaking out into recipe files everywhere.

This is the recipe, more or less, that gave my friends and me such a delicious thrill when we shared it (not to mention tasted the result). The restaurant, I'm told, still exists, though in a different location and under a different management. Perhaps they no longer make the cheesecake, or if they do, they surely know by now that the word has gotten out: the recipe is from Kraft and has been widely published. This homemade version (the model, it

seems to me, for the most popular brand of frozen cheesecake), free from flour or other gummy thickeners, is moist, light, tender and tangy from a good squeeze of fresh lemon juice. Garnish each slice with a perfect strawberry.

1	cup graham cracker crumbs
3	tablespoons sugar
3	tablespoons margarine, melted
	* * *
2	8-oz. pkgs. PHILADELPHIA BRAND Cream Cheese
½	cup sugar
1	tablespoon lemon juice
1	teaspoon grated lemon rind
½	teaspoon vanilla
2	eggs, separated
	* * *
1	cup dairy sour cream
2	tablespoons sugar
1	teaspoon vanilla

Combine crumbs, sugar and margarine; press onto bottom of 9-inch springform pan. Bake at 325°, 10 minutes.

Combine softened cream cheese, sugar, lemon juice, rind and vanilla, mixing at medium speed on electric mixer until well blended. Add egg yolks, one at a time, mixing well after each addition. Fold in stiffly beaten egg whites; pour over crust. Bake at 300°, 45 minutes.

10 to 12 servings

Combine sour cream, sugar and vanilla. Carefully spread over cheesecake; continue baking 10 minutes. Loosen cake from rim of pan; cool before removing rim of pan. Chill.

PINA COLADA CAKE

Coconut: You are either fer it or agin' it, and the country seems about equally divided between those who can't get enough of the sweet, nutty stuff and those who, when they find a coconut-filled candy in a box of assorted chocolates, spit the offender into the nearest potted plant.

The appeal (for those who feel it) is at least partly based on the exotic, tropical island mystery coconut evokes. The most intense form of the experience may well be the product called cream of coconut—a thick, sweet coco-concentrated syrup that tastes of pure coconut (please don't read the list of ingredients). Although a cocktail called piña colada ("strained pineapple" in Spanish) existed as early as the Twenties, the first recorded brand of coconut cream, Coco Lopez®, was introduced in 1948, and shortly thereafter the rum, pineapple and coconut cream cocktail as we know it was created.

In the great American tradition of turning cocktails into desserts, here is a cake inspired by, and packed with the essential ingredients for, that tall, tropical cooler. Serve it at your next luau.

1	(18⅓–18½-ounce) package yellow cake mix*
1	(4-serving size) package *instant* vanilla flavor pudding mix
1	(15-ounce) can COCO LOPEZ® Cream of Coconut
½	cup plus 2 tablespoons rum
⅓	cup vegetable oil
4	eggs
1	(8-ounce) can crushed pineapple, *well-drained* Pineapple chunks, maraschino cherries, toasted coconut for garnish, optional Coconut Cream Sauce

Preheat oven to 350°. In large mixer bowl, combine cake mix, pudding mix, *½ cup* cream of coconut, *½ cup* rum, oil and eggs. Beat on medium speed 2 minutes. Stir in pineapple. Pour into well-greased and floured 10-inch fluted or tube pan. Bake 50 to 55 minutes. Cool 10 minutes. Remove from pan. With a table knife or skewer, poke holes about 1 inch apart in cake almost to bottom. Combine remaining cream of coconut and remaining *2 tablespoons* rum; slowly spoon over cake. Chill thoroughly. Garnish. Serve with Coconut Cream Sauce. Store in refrigerator.

COCONUT CREAM SAUCE: In small mixer bowl, combine 1 cup (½ pint) BORDEN® Whipping Cream and ½ cup cream of coconut: beat *only* until stiff. Sauce can be held in refrigerator 2 to 3 hours. (Makes about 2 cups)

*If cake mix with "pudding in" is used, omit pudding mix.

GELATIN POKE CAKE

The earliest patent for a "potable" gelatin-based instant food was issued in 1845, but not until the Postum Cereal Company purchased the rights to Jell-O® in 1923 did the wiggly dessert begin to achieve true national prominence. Today the Jell-O® test kitchens boast some 1,700 recipes that use the product. These creations range from pizza to popcorn, plus, of course, plenty of layered, molded, rearranged and otherwise manipulated gelatin desserts and salads. While there are still people who eat their Jell-O® plain (hence those whipped topping-dolloped dishes of quivering multicolored cubes prominently displayed on the Connor family's kitchen table during the opening credits of *Roseanne*), turning mere gelatin into something more dramatic seems to be part of the basic appeal.

One altogether odd but endearing production number is this cake, with its internal bath of Jell-O®. Poked full of holes, which allow the unset gelatin to seep throughout, the cake has many fans. Try it—the guarantee is you've never eaten anything quite like it before.

1   package (2-layer size) white cake mix or pudding-included cake mix
1   package (4-serving size) JELL-O® Gelatin, any flavor
1   cup boiling water
½   cup cold water
3½ cups (8 oz.) COOL WHIP® Non-Dairy Whipped Topping, thawed

Prepare cake batter as directed on package, and pour into well-greased and floured 13 × 9-inch pan. Bake at 350° for 30 to 35 minutes, or until cake tester inserted in center comes out clean. Cool cake in pan 15 minutes; then pierce with utility fork at ½-inch intervals.

Meanwhile, dissolve gelatin in boiling water. Add cold water and carefully pour over cake. Chill 3 to 4 hours. Garnish with whipped topping and fruit or Marzipan, if desired.

In high altitude areas, follow package directions for cake mix.

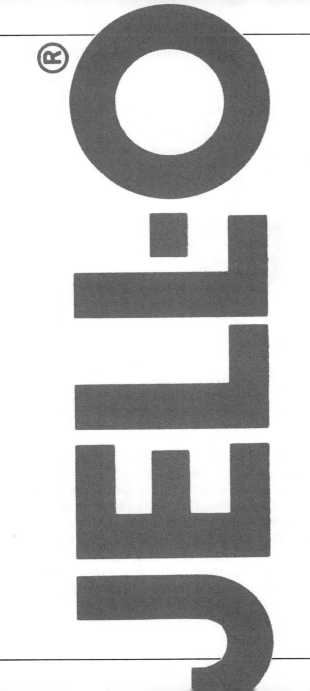

ALTERNATE BAKING PANS:

One 10-inch tube pan for 45 to 50 minutes; remove from pan and place on waxed paper before adding gelatin.

Two 8-inch or 9-inch layer pans for 30 to 35 minutes; remove from pans and place in clean pans or on waxed paper before adding gelatin. Fill and frost with 3½ cups (8 oz.) COOL WHIP® Non-Dairy Whipped Topping, thawed.

PIES: A LITTLE WEDGE OF PARADISE

If cakes are magic, pies are sculpture and equally scary to those of us whose manual dexterity is shaky. It's frustrating, since there's just no dessert like a warm, luscious homemade pie, cooling (at least in our imaginations) on the sill of a lace-curtained window. Such baking abilities were long used to judge a woman's suitability for marrying (Billy Boy, Billy Boy), a state of affairs the frozen pie folks made obsolete. Factory pies, hot and bubbly from the oven, are fabulous fakes. With plenty of sense-memory and a generous dose of cosmetic whipped topping, they can almost be passed off as genuine. Nowadays a real pie is rare, and marriages are made for other reasons, but there is still no substitute for homemade.

Long before the freezer replaced the oven, the back of the box was the place to turn for great pie recipes. Once a cook could make a tender, flaky crust (admittedly the hard part, and still a skill best learned directly from Mom), the filling was almost easy. If not fresh fruit, a little sugar and spice and a pat of butter, then one of the following time-tested pies, each and every one still worth marrying someone for.

FROZEN STRAWBERRY-YOGURT PIE

A frozen pie is like a savings bond—one day it's suddenly worth more than you ever thought possible, particularly with unexpected company (or just an everyday scheduling snafu) to contend with. Knowing a pie is waiting in the bank, as it were, lets you relax all smug and enjoy your just desserts.

2	containers (8 oz. each) vanilla yogurt
3½	cups thawed COOL WHIP® Non-Dairy Whipped Topping, or COOL WHIP® Extra Creamy Dairy Recipe Whipped Topping*
2	cups sweetened diced, sliced or finely chopped strawberries
1	baked 9-inch graham cracker crumb crust, or pie shell, cooled

Fold yogurt into whipped topping, blend well; fold in strawberries. Spoon into crust. (Or, spoon yogurt mixture and strawberries alternately into crust. Cut through with spatula to marble.) Freeze until firm, 4 hours or overnight.

Remove from freezer 30 minutes before serving and keep chilled in refrigerator. Garnish with additional whole strawberries, if desired.

Store any leftover pie in freezer.

*Or use 2 envelopes DREAM WHIP® Whipped Topping mix or D-ZERTA® Reduced Calorie Whipped Topping, prepared as directed on package.

LIBBY'S® FAMOUS PUMPKIN PIE

Pumpkin pie, it is said, was served at the very first Thanksgiving feast. This is apocryphal but possible, since American Indians did eat pumpkins and other squash, and the English were great bakers of pies. Certainly by 1796, when the first known pumpkin pie recipe was published, the dessert was already an established Thanksgiving tradition.

In 1929, when Libby, McNeil & Libby acquired The Dickinson Canning Company, a small manufacturer of pumpkin puree, the pie took another giant step forward. The recipe was streamlined, polished and fine tuned to make baking it as easy as, well, as pie. Nowadays, of course, few Thanksgiving menus are complete without one of the handsome brown-and-orange pies waiting on the sideboard.

This classic is always on the Libby's® can, but since no back-of-the-box collection would be complete without it and because some people apparently mash their own pumpkin puree, here is the recipe. Such pumpkin pioneers may get great satisfaction from huffing and puffing the retired Halloween jack o'lantern through a sieve, but the truth is Libby's® exclusive hybrid pumpkin— the richly flavored, meaty Dickinson—makes a puree that's almost impossible to duplicate at home.

1   *unbaked* 9-inch (4-cup volume) pie crust
2   eggs, lightly beaten

1¾   cups (16-ounce can) LIBBY'S ® Solid Pack Pumpkin
¾   cup granulated sugar
½   teaspoon salt
1   teaspoon ground cinnamon
½   teaspoon ground ginger
¼   teaspoon ground cloves
1½   cups (12-ounce can) *undiluted* CARNATION® Evaporated Milk

In large bowl, combine eggs, pumpkin, sugar, salt, cinnamon, ginger, cloves, and evaporated milk. Pour into pie crust.* Bake in preheated 425°F oven for 15 minutes. Reduce temperature to 350°F. Bake an additional 40 to 50 minutes, or until knife inserted near center comes out clean. Cool on wire rack. Top pie as desired. Makes one 9-inch pie.

NOTE: When using metal or foil pie pan, bake on preheated cookie sheet. When using glass or ceramic pie plate, do not use cookie sheet.

GILDING THE LILY: A couple of tablespoons of bourbon or dark rum, added to the pie or the whipped cream, is a nice touch. For sweet potato pie, replace the pumpkin with an equal quantity (1½ cups) of cooked, pureed sweet potatoes, or yams. For a crisper bottom crust, bake the pie on a cookie sheet that has been left in the oven during preheating.

MOCK APPLE PIE

Pastry for two-crust 9-inch pie
36 RITZ® Crackers, coarsely broken (about 1¾ cups crumbs)
2   cups water
2   cups sugar
2   teaspoons cream of tartar
2   tablespoons lemon juice
    Grated rind of one lemon
2   tablespoons BLUE BONNET® Margarine
½   teaspoon ground cinnamon

Many have heard of this back-of-the-box oddity, but few have actually sampled it. It is said to be a Depression era version of an earlier pie originally made with plain crackers or even hardtack, which dated back to the Civil War. War or Depression, it's hard to imagine why there would be crackers but not apples in distribution. Nabisco® admits a little sheepishly that they have considered just making up some other, more logical reason for the eccentric pastry's existence, but for now they are content to render a corporate shrug when pressed for details. Certainly Mock Apple Pie, baked in a scratch crust and served warm with a diversionary scoop of ice cream or a wedge of cheddar cheese, tastes (or more accurately *feels*) much like the real thing. While it may be a timesaver for those who hate to peel apples, and it's a natural on April Fool's Day, the real excuse for baking it may be—like climbing Mt. Everest—the simple satisfaction of knowing you can.

Roll out half the pastry and line a 9-inch pie plate. Place cracker crumbs in prepared crust. In saucepan, over high heat, heat water, sugar and cream of tartar to a boil; simmer for 15 minutes. Add lemon juice and rind; cool. Pour syrup over cracker crumbs. Dot with margarine; sprinkle with cinnamon. Roll out remaining pastry; place over pie. Trim, seal and flute edges. Slit top crust to allow steam to escape.

Bake at 425°F for 30 to 35 minutes or until crust is crisp and golden. Serve warm. Makes 8 servings

KEY LIME PIE

Natives of the Florida Keys have streamlined lime pie-making to a fine art, enabling them to sell as many slices of pie to as many tourists as possible while the season lasts. The lime trees, which for the lucky few produce an abundant—and free—windfall of the small, mildly tangy fruit, are unique to the Keys.

This recipe, from Borden® (slightly different from the ubiquitous postcard version sold everywhere south of Miami), proves you don't actually need a key lime tree—or even a fresh lime—and you certainly don't have to trek any further than the kitchen cupboard when the mood strikes. Some versions are meringue-topped, but connoisseurs prefer whipped cream.

1   (9- or 10-inch) baked pastry shell *or* graham cracker crumb crust
6   egg yolks*
2   (14-ounce) cans EAGLE® Brand Sweetened Condensed Milk (NOT evaporated milk)
1   (8-ounce) bottle REALIME® Lime Juice from Concentrate
     Green food coloring, optional
     Whipped cream or whipped topping

Preheat oven to 350°. In large mixer bowl, beat egg yolks with sweetened condensed milk. Stir in REALIME® Brand and food coloring if desired. Pour into prepared pastry shell; bake 12 minutes. Cool. Chill. Top with whipped cream. Garnish as desired. Refrigerate leftovers.

Makes one 9- or 10-inch pie

*Use only Grade A clean, uncracked eggs.

DELUXE PECAN PIE

Sometimes the best back-of-the-package formulas aren't odd, unique or gimmicky in any way. Instead, they are merely the ideal version of an already popular recipe, polished to perfection by the test kitchen in question. This pecan pie is just such a recipe, adapted to use corn syrup in place of the molasses traditionally called for in the Deep South. Karo® won't take credit for first making the switch, but they are rightfully proud of this classically proportioned recipe, which will enable you to turn out a pecan pie that is sweet, sticky perfection.

3   eggs, slightly beaten
1   cup KARO® Light or Dark Corn Syrup
1   cup sugar
2   tablespoons MAZOLA® Margarine, melted
1   teaspoon vanilla
1½   cups pecans
1   unbaked (9-inch) pastry shell

In medium bowl, stir together eggs, corn syrup, sugar, margarine and vanilla until well blended. Stir in pecans. Pour into pastry shell. Bake in 350°F oven 50 to 55 minutes or until knife inserted halfway between center and edge comes out clean. Cool on wire rack. If desired, serve with whipped cream. Makes 1 (9-inch) pie.

GILDING THE LILY: The pecans can be increased to 2 cups. The sugar can be decreased to ½ cup. One tablespoon molasses and 1 tablespoon bourbon or dark rum can be added to the filling. To make maple-flavored pecan pie, substitute KARO® Pancake and Waffle Syrup for the corn syrup.

LEMON MERINGUE PIE

In the early Eighties, when this simply perfect pie recipe came off the Argo® and Kingsford's® Corn Starch boxes, all hell broke loose—a classic tale of back-of-the-package panic. So long had the trusty formula appeared on the packages, few had thought to clip and save it, and after it vanished, many went to bed hungry for lemon pie before it finally reappeared. Consumer affairs people at CPC International still remember this Dark Age of lemon meringue pie with appropriate horror (they, after all, answer the phones and mail out the thousands of recipe requests). While it seems fairly safe to say the recipe is now on the box for good, it is printed here, just in case.

1	cup sugar
3	tablespoons ARGO® or KINGSFORD'S® Corn Starch
1½	cups cold water
3	egg yolks, slightly beaten
	Grated rind of 1 lemon
¼	cup lemon juice
1	tablespoon MAZOLA® Margarine
1	baked (9-inch) pastry shell
3	egg whites, at room temperature
⅓	cup sugar

In 2-quart saucepan, stir together 1 cup sugar and corn starch. Gradually stir in water until smooth. Stir in egg yolks. Stirring constantly, bring to boil over medium heat and boil 1 minute. Remove from heat. Stir in next 3 ingredients. Cool. Turn into pastry shell. In small bowl with mixer at high speed beat egg whites until foamy. Gradually beat in ⅓ cup sugar; continue beating until stiff peaks form. Spread some meringue around edge of filling first, touching crust all around, then fill in center. Bake in 350°F oven 15 to 20 minutes or until lightly browned. Cool. Serves 6 to 8.

GILDING THE LILY: For Creamy Lemon Pie replace the water with cold milk. To make a lemon-lime pie, replace half of lemon juice with lime juice; add grated rind of 1 lime to the grated lemon rind.

COOKIES: THE TOLL HOUSE AND BEYOND

Cookies mean caring. A happy holdover from childhood, they are the ultimate treat, eaten simply for the pleasure of the eating. Grabbed warm from a baking sheet or filched from a poorly hidden cookie jar, they entice small and tall kids alike.

Cookies have been with us for centuries. At first they were flat cakes, sweetened with honey, baked as an offering for the gods. When savvy ancients realized that a few sweetened cakes could be held back for mortal consumption, man had passed an important milestone in civilization. From the Dutch word for small cake *(koekje),* cookies are now celebrated in America as they are in no other country.

From utilitarian chocolate-dipped pretzels to swank almond streusel-topped raspberry bars; from standard habit-forming store-bought chocolate sandwich cookies to yupwardly mobile white chocolate-macadamia chunks; from buttery little sophisticated mouthfuls to gooey deep-dish pizza pans of chocolaty bliss, cookies run the gamut of sweet happiness.

While it has become increasingly unnecessary to bake cookies at home—as computerized robotic baking installations have picked up the slack from Mom—those who still believe the ideal cookie is fresh, warm and handmade know one of the best sources for such recipes is the back of the box. Cookie gourmets have an astonishing abundance of foolproof formulas to choose from; among them are these classics.

CRISP PEANUT BUTTER COOKIES

SKIPPY®

Peanut butter has been around since the turn of the century; Skippy® since 1923. Some 700 million pounds of peanut butter are consumed annually in the U.S. and while most of it no doubt goes into p.b. and j. sandwiches, a goodly share also gets baked into these crisp, classic cookies, complete with the traditional cross-hatching (produced by flattening the cookies with the tines of a fork).

2½	cups unsifted flour
1	teaspoon baking powder
1	teaspoon baking soda
¼	teaspoon salt
1	cup MAZOLA® Margarine
1	cup SKIPPY® Creamy or Super Chunk™ Peanut Butter
1	cup sugar
1	cup firmly packed brown sugar
2	eggs
1	teaspoon vanilla

In small bowl stir flour, baking powder, baking soda and salt. In large bowl with mixer at medium speed, beat margarine and peanut butter until smooth. Beat in sugars until blended. Beat in eggs and vanilla. Add flour mixture; beat until well blended. If necessary, refrigerate dough. Shape into 1-inch balls. Place 2 inches apart on ungreased cookie sheets. Flatten with fork dipped in sugar making crisscross pattern. Bake in 350°F oven 12 minutes or until lightly browned. Remove from cookie sheets. Cool completely on wire rack. Store in tightly covered container. Makes 6 dozen.

GILDING THE LILY: For Orange Peanut Butter Cookies, add 1 tablespoon grated fresh orange rind with the eggs. Six to 12 ounces of semisweet chocolate chips can be added to the dough. The cookies can be partially dipped into melted semisweet chocolate.

TOLL HOUSE® COOKIES

Unlike most of the best-known back-of-the-box recipes, this all-American cookie classic began long ago and far away from any corporate test kitchen. In 1930, at The Toll House Inn, in Whitman, Massachusetts, Ruth Wakefield chopped a milk chocolate bar into chunks and stirred them into a batch of dough for her Butter Drop-Dos. She assumed that during the baking the chocolate would melt and mix throughout the dough. She wanted chocolate cookies. What she got were chocolate chunk cookies.

With typical New England frugality, she served them anyway, and the cookies were a hit. She renamed them Chocolate Crispies, and when the recipe appeared in a Boston newspaper, regional sales of chocolate bars boomed. The chocolate maker (Nestlé®) first responded by producing a small tool designed to cut chocolate bars into chunks, and then turned out a chocolate bar already scored to break apart into small bits.

Such moments of food destiny can only be appreciated in retrospect. Who can imagine a world without chocolate chip cookies? Without David Liederman, Mrs. Fields and Famous Wally Amos? What, no Keebler elves?

Fortunately, Nestlé® bowled to the inevitable with commendable mercenary grace, and in 1939 bought the Toll House name and began manufacturing the semisweet chocolate "morsels" we bake with today.

After 40 years (and uncounted tons of warm cookies washed down with untold gallons of ice-cold milk), Nestlé®'s original agreement with The Toll House Inn expired. They were now allowed to alter the original recipe, and did so slightly, eliminating the directions to sift the flour, omitting the tiny amount of water called for, shortening the baking time by two minutes, and omitting the need to grease the baking sheets.

These minute changes were in response to modern ingredients and modern impatience to cut to the chase—in this case, a molten chipper snarfed straight from the cookie sheet. Tampering with a successful back-of-the-box formula is a tricky business, akin to omitting one altogether, but for the most part Nestlé®'s changes have been well received. A few crotchety duffers insist the *original* original makes the better cookie, and in the interests of thoroughness (leaving no morsel unbaked) here are both. Finally, for those who are too impatient to "drop by teaspoonfuls" or who have a major bake sale contribution to produce, there is the even simpler pan variation—a truly streamlined version of what is surely America's most popular cookie.

THE *ORIGINAL* ORIGINAL TOLL HOUSE® COOKIES

1   cup plus 2 tbsps. sifted flour
½   tsp. baking soda
½   tsp. salt
½   cup soft butter or shortening.
6   Tbsps. granulated sugar
6   Tbsps. firmly packed brown sugar
½   tsp. vanilla
¼   tsp. water
1   egg
1   package (1 cup) NESTLÉ® TOLL HOUSE®
        Semi-Sweet Chocolate Morsels
½   cup coarsely chopped walnuts

Sift together flour, baking soda, salt; set aside.
Combine in bowl butter, granulated and brown
sugars, vanilla and water; beat until creamy. Beat
in egg. Add flour mixture and mix well. Stir in
chocolate morsels and walnuts. Drop by well-
rounded half teaspoonfuls onto greased cookie
sheet.

BAKE at: 375°F   TIME: 10 to 12 minutes.

Makes: 50 cookies

THE *OFFICIAL* ORIGINAL TOLL HOUSE® COOKIES

2¼   cups all-purpose flour
1   measuring teaspoon baking soda
1   measuring teaspoon salt
1   cup butter, softened
¾   cup sugar
¾   cup firmly packed brown sugar
1   measuring teaspoon vanilla extract
2   eggs
1   12-oz. pkg. (2 cups) NESTLÉ® TOLL HOUSE®
        Semi-Sweet Chocolate Morsels
1   cup chopped nuts

Preheat oven to 375°F. In small bowl, combine flour,
baking soda and salt; set aside. In large bowl,
combine butter, sugar, brown sugar and vanilla extract;
beat until creamy. Beat in eggs. Gradually add flour
mixture. Stir in NESTLÉ® TOLL HOUSE® Semi-Sweet
Chocolate Morsels and nuts. Drop by level measuring
tablespoonfuls onto ungreased cookie sheets.

BAKE at: 375°F.   TIME: 9–11 minutes

Makes: 5 dozen cookies

THE PAN COOKIE VARIATION

Spread dough into greased 15½ × 10½ × 1-inch
baking pan. Bake at 375°F. for 20–25 minutes.
Cool completely. Cut into thirty-five 2-inch squares.

GILDING THE LILY: Use white or bittersweet
chocolate; use chocolate chunks or jumbo chips;
use dark brown sugar; use pecans, cashews or
macadamia nuts; for a softer cookie, replace the
butter with shortening and decrease the baking
time by 2 minutes. For jumbo cookies, drop the
dough by rounded tablespoons and extend the
baking time 2 to 3 minutes.

QUAKER'S® BEST OATMEAL COOKIES

When an American cookie *meister* thinks of an oatmeal cookie, this is the version that comes to mind. There is no recorded date for the first addition of oats to cookies, but this recipe has been on the Quaker® box since 1955. Like many back-of-the-box formulas, it is believed that this is a perfected version of a recipe already popular before it came to corporate attention. If you are quick on your feet when getting them out of the oven, these are cookies that can supply the best parts of both crisp and soft (the kind, in fact, called chewy, that the packaged-cookie people failed so miserably at a few years ago), a cookie, in short, worthy of being called both "best" and "famous." Maybe even "perfect."

1¼ cups margarine
¾   cup firmly packed brown sugar
½   cup granulated sugar
1   egg
1   teaspoon vanilla
1½ cups all-purpose flour
1   teaspoon baking soda
1   teaspoon salt (optional)
1   teaspoon cinnamon (optional)
¼   teaspoon nutmeg (optional)
3   cups QUAKER® Oats (Quick or Old Fashioned, uncooked)

Heat oven to 375°F. Beat together margarine and sugars until light and fluffy. Beat in egg and vanilla. Combine flour, baking soda, salt and spices; add to margarine mixture, mixing well. Stir in oats. Drop by rounded tablespoonfuls onto ungreased cookie sheet. Bake 8 to 9 minutes for a chewy cookie, 10 to 11 minutes for a crisp cookie. Cool 1 minute on cookie sheet; remove to wire cooling rack. Store in tightly covered container.

4½ DOZEN

VARIATIONS: Add any one or combination of two of the following ingredients, if desired: 1 cup raisins, chopped nuts, or semi-sweet chocolate, butterscotch or peanut butter flavored pieces.

COCONUT MACAROONS

Coconut lovers surely know this recipe by heart—the tiny, toasted morsels of intense coconut flavor are irresistible, and the recipe is utterly simple to prepare.

2   (7-ounce) packages *flaked* coconut (5⅓ cups)
1   (14-ounce) can EAGLE® Brand Sweetened
        Condensed Milk (NOT evaporated milk)
2   teaspoons vanilla extract
1½   teaspoons almond extract

Preheat oven to 350°. In large bowl, combine coconut, sweetened condensed milk and extracts; mix well. Drop by rounded teaspoonfuls onto aluminum foil-lined and *generously greased* baking sheets; garnish as desired. Bake 8 to 10 minutes or until lightly browned around edges. *Immediately* remove from baking sheets (macaroons will stick if allowed to cool). Store loosely covered at room temperature.

Makes about 4 dozen

MACAROON KISSES: Prepare and bake as above. Press solid milk chocolate candy drops in center of each macaroon immediately after baking.

CHERRY NUT: Omit almond extract. Add 1 cup chopped nuts and 2 tablespoons maraschino cherry syrup. Press maraschino cherry half into center of each macaroon before baking.

OLD-FASHIONED HERMITS

Old-fashioned is the right term for this simple recipe, dating back to Sun Maid's® 1923 cookbook. The general notion of a soft spice cookie chock-full of dried fruit and nuts is many years older than that, though, with such regional additions as sour cream or molasses contributing to the moist texture and rich flavor. The recipe has many variations, but the name, like most nonsense monickers we apply to cookies, has stuck. Back when all factory cookies were necessarily crisp—if not downright hard—in order to survive the rigors of distribution, Hermits and their tender cousins were the epitome of homemade. They still are.

2	cups all-purpose flour
2	teaspoons baking powder
1	teaspoon cinnamon
½	teaspoon nutmeg
¼	teaspoon cloves
¼	teaspoon salt
½	cup shortening
½	cup granulated sugar
½	cup packed brown sugar
2	eggs
1	cup SUN MAID® Raisins
¾	cup chopped DIAMOND® Walnuts

Sift together flour, baking powder, spices and salt. Cream shortening, sugars, and eggs together well. Blend in flour mixture. Add raisins and walnuts; mix well. Drop by teaspoonfuls onto greased baking sheets. Bake at 350 degrees F. for 12 to 15 minutes or until lightly browned. Makes about 3 dozen cookies.

RICE KRISPIES TREATS®

® Kellogg Company

There can be no denying the easy appeal of a cookie or bar that requires no baking. This back-of-the-box favorite, developed in the 1940s, has long been a staple in houses where ravenous kids, sudden company or midnight hungries disrupt otherwise well-laid plans. As with many of the most enduring and effective back-of-the-box formulas, it almost seems as if these treats have usurped the original purpose of the product in question. I know there must be people who eat Rice Krispies® for breakfast, but who and where are they? Three ingredients (good keepers all), two pans and about 5 minutes of work are all it takes to create this sweet, spontaneous snack.

¼ cup margarine or butter
1 10-ounce package (about 40) regular marshmallows *or* 4 cups miniature marshmallows
5 cups KELLOGG'S® RICE KRISPIES® cereal

Melt margarine in large saucepan over low heat. Add marshmallows and stir until completely melted; remove from heat.

Add KELLOGG'S® RICE KRISPIES® cereal, stirring until well coated.

Using buttered spatula or waxed paper, press mixture evenly into buttered 13 × 9 × 2-inch pan. Cut into 2-inch squares.

YIELD: 24 squares

NOTE: Use fresh marshmallows for best results.

GILDING THE LILY: Stir 1 cup raisins or 1 cup peanuts (or a combination) into the mixture along with the cereal. Stir ¼ cup peanut butter into the marshmallow mixture just before adding the cereal.

CHEWY CHOCOLATE COOKIES

The Reese®'s Peanut Butter Cup, which celebrates the affinity between peanuts and chocolate more successfully than almost any other American confection, was first produced in 1923, in Hershey, Pennsylvania. Eventually acquired by Hershey, the trademark is also applied to Reese®'s Pieces® (famed thanks to "E.T.") and Reese®'s Peanut Butter Chips. These chocolate cookies, of the soft and chewy persuasion, include plenty of those chips (Reese®'s Pieces® Candy can be substituted) and do as well by the chocolate-peanut butter partnership as the original inspiration ever did. Phone home, and ask someone to bake you a batch.

1¼	cups butter or margarine, softened
2	cups sugar
2	eggs
2	teaspoons vanilla extract
2	cups all-purpose flour
¾	cup HERSHEY®'S Cocoa
1	teaspoon baking soda
½	teaspoon salt
2	cups (12-ounce package) REESE®'S Peanut Butter Chips

Heat oven to 350°. Cream butter and sugar until light and fluffy. Add eggs and vanilla; beat well. Combine flour, cocoa, baking soda and salt; gradually blend into creamed mixture. Stir in chips. Drop by teaspoonfuls onto ungreased cookie sheet. Bake 8 to 9 minutes. (Do not overbake; cookies will be soft. They will puff while baking and flatten while cooling.) Cool slightly; remove from cookie sheet onto wire rack. Cool completely. About 4½ dozen cookies.

PAN RECIPE:

Spread peanut butter chip-chocolate batter in greased 15½ × 10½ × 1-inch jelly-roll pan. Bake at 350° for 20 minutes or until set. Cool completely; cut into bars. About 4 dozen bars.

GORP BARS

If solid rocket fuel contained marshmallows and was edible, it would probably be Gorp Bars. Based upon the granola-like trail snack carried by many healthy, mellow trekkers of the Sixties, the bars were apparently intended to deliver long-lasting high fat, high fiber, high calorie energy to cross-country skiers, mountain climbers and trans-Antarctic explorers. Gorp Bars will also drive the children into a sugary frenzy—and with relatively little kitchen time on your part. In short, if you ever go trick-or-treating at NASA, expect to end up with Gorp Bars in your goodie bag.

Seriously, though, this intensely concentrated little food, bristling with assorted crunchy things and spangled with colored candies and raisins, is so easy to make, satisfying to chew and so solidly portable, you'll find lots of reasons to add it to lunch boxes, brown bags, or any other meal eaten on the run.

2	cups bite-size crispy corn cereal squares
2½	cups thin pretzel sticks, broken in half
1½	cups M&M's® Peanut Chocolate Candies
1	cup unsalted banana chips
¾	cup golden raisins
½	cup butter or margarine
⅓	cup creamy peanut butter
1	bag (10-oz.) marshmallows

In large bowl, combine cereal, pretzels, candies, banana chips, and raisins. In medium saucepan, melt together butter, peanut butter, and marshmallows. Stir over low heat until mixture is smooth. Immediately pour mixture over cereal, mixing until cereal and other ingredients are thoroughly coated. Press lightly into greased 13 × 9-inch pan. Let stand until firm. Cut into bars to serve.

MAKES ONE 13 × 9 inch PAN OF BAR COOKIES.

HINT: One 16-ounce package equals 2¼ cups.

GILDING THE LILY: Substitute dried cherries, dried blueberries or dried cranberries (craisins) for the golden raisins; replace the Peanut Chocolate Candies with 1 cup regular M&M's® and add ½ cup chopped almonds, cashews or walnuts.

PUDDINGS: TENDER IS THE BITE

Puddings recall a time of uncomplicated childhood, free from adult worries and genuine hardship, when bad things were easily banished by the cool comfort of a spoonful or two of pudding. Deep chocolate, tender tapioca, rich butterscotch, raisin-studded rice—at one time or another they soothed sore tonsils, spelling bee defeats, even the imagined heartache of young love, and became a kind of emotional band-aid that Mother instinctively knew when to apply.

Despite their apparent sweet simplicity, any grown-up cook knows that puddings can be unreliable. Like other egg-thickened concoctions, they take some watching, and they can scorch and curdle, or turn out too thick, lumpy, *odd.* Even sweaty, vigilant stirring over a closely watched pot is no guarantee of silky, tender success. Quick, convenient packaged pudding mixes long ago replaced scratch versions in most American homes, and while Jell-O® Pudding can now actually be purchased ready-made, reducing the guesswork even further, there's still considerable consolation to be found in the sight of a pudding being stirred—however briefly—on the stove.

Such shortcut puddings seem heaven sent, and uncomplicated palates will find the expected comfort in eating them. Over the years pudding mixes have also been included in some very successful back-of-the-package formulas, frequently embellished into ornate but reliable desserts that stretch the meaning of mere pudding. Other back-of-the box puddings rely on unexpected ingredients (cereal, packaged cookies) or less skittish thickeners (corn starch) for their odd appeal, but the results remain lovably simple and sweet— casual desserts after simple meals, or perfect snacks whenever being grown-up gets too hard to bear.

BANANA PUDDING

This soft, sweet cookie/pudding/custard combination originated in the Deep South, where bananas and desserts are taken very seriously indeed. It was not developed by Nabisco®, but instead was adapted from an existing popular recipe to use Nabisco's® Nilla® Wafers. If you have had one of several ornate French dessert concoctions, called charlottes, prepared in a mold lined and layered with ladyfingers, or have sampled a genuine English trifle, you will recognize the general evolutionary path this pudding has taken. Today, when occasional attempts are made to modernize the rather old-fashioned formula (by using pudding mixes, for example) angry letters from loyal consumers protest the alteration of a classic.

Democratically, the pudding shows up in both linen-and-silver restaurants (oftentimes transformed into an elegant pie, tart or cake) and at rural all-you-can-hold eateries, turned out in enormous, labor-saving steam-table pans. In a Carolina barbecue house (an excellent example of the latter) thoughts of tucking into another rack of hickory-smoked ribs may tempt you to abandon dessert. Experience, however, suggests that when banana pudding is on the buffet, as it usually is, you would be well advised to save room.

¾	cup granulated sugar
3	tablespoons all-purpose flour
	dash of salt
4	eggs
2	cups milk
½	teaspoon vanilla extract
	NILLA® Wafers
5-6	medium size fully ripe bananas, sliced

Combine ½ cup sugar, flour and salt in top of double boiler. Mix in 1 whole egg and 3 egg yolks. Stir in milk. Cook, uncovered, over boiling water, stirring constantly, until thickened. Remove from heat; add vanilla. Spread small amount on bottom of 1½-quart casserole; cover with layer of NILLA® Wafers. Top with layer of sliced bananas. Pour about ⅓ of custard over bananas. Continue to layer wafers, bananas, and custard to make 3 layers of each ending with custard. Beat remaining 3 egg whites stiff, but not dry; gradually add remaining ¼ cup sugar and beat until mixture forms stiff peaks. Pile on top of pudding covering entire surface. Bake in preheated hot oven (425°F) 5 minutes or until delicately browned. Serve warm or chilled. Makes 8 servings

OLD-FASHIONED RICE PUDDING

Controversy swirls around this nursery-simple dessert, proving Americans can care as passionately about food as any Frenchman. Should the rice be cooked in the pudding or cooked separately and added to the thickened custard? Should there be raisins (I say yes, and I say lots) or not (someone once told me they look like bugs). Is rice pudding served warm or cold? Is cinnamon an option, or an essential? Tough questions with no easy answers.

While the debate rages, let's sample some pudding, made from this quick and easy recipe that has enough options built in to make even the fussiest connoisseur happy. In fact, despite the multiple convenience products involved, this version tastes surprisingly like that found in diners (*good* diners), where rice pudding is taken as seriously as any other dessert. You know the diner puddings I mean, portioned into stout little ceramic custard cups and waiting, along with the meringue pies, in one of those refrigerated cases with the tilted mirror, the kind that lets you spend your entire meal eye-balling the sweet contents and planning your inevitable dessert. I'll have rice pudding and a refill on this coffee, please.

4　cups cold milk
1　cup MINUTE RICE®
1　package (4-servings size) JELL-O® Vanilla or Coconut Cream Flavor Pudding and Pie Filling
¼　cup raisins (optional)
1　egg, well beaten
¼　teaspoon ground cinnamon
⅛　teaspoon ground nutmeg

Combine milk, rice, pudding mix, raisins and egg in medium saucepan. Bring to a full boil over medium heat, stirring constantly. Remove from heat. Cool 5 minutes, stirring twice. Pour into individual dessert dishes or serving bowl. Sprinkle with cinnamon and nutmeg; serve warm. (For chilled pudding, place plastic wrap directly on hot pudding. Cool slightly; chill about 1 hour. Stir before serving; sprinkle with cinnamon and nutmeg.)

Makes 10 servings

OLD-FASHIONED FRUIT RICE PUDDING: Add 1 can (17½ oz.) drained fruit cocktail to pudding after cooling 5 minutes. Garnish as desired.

GILDING THE LILY: Better cold than hot, this pudding can use more raisins than called for, and is also good with some of the more exotic dried fruit now on the market—blueberries, cherries, cranberries.

ALL-TIME FAVORITE PUFF PUDDING

Grape-Nuts® has been around since 1898, when it joined the earliest generation of manufactured American cereals (among them Kellogg's® Toasted Corn Flakes and Post's® Elijah's Mann, later renamed Post Toasties®). When the cereal is baked in this two-layer pudding, the distinctively nutty wheat and barley taste remains, but the texture turns tender and nubbly. For years Grape-Nuts® pudding struck me as nothing more than a hard-times dessert, something to whip up when the larder and the bank account were fairly bare, but I sampled it recently at one of Boston's toniest seafood restaurants, and came away with a whole new respect for the simple, frugal concoction. Certainly there was a cost-conscious New England spirit about it, but far from feeling like the times were hard (after all, I had just eaten a lobster the size of a Great Dane), I felt remarkably well taken care of, and I encourage you to take advantage of the following formula the next time you need coddling.

¼	cup (½ stick) butter or margarine
½	cup sugar or honey
1	teaspoon grated lemon rind
2	egg yolks
3	tablespoons lemon juice
2	tablespoons all-purpose flour
¼	cup POST® GRAPE-NUTS® or Raisin GRAPE-NUTS® Brand Cereal*
1	cup milk
2	egg whites, stiffly beaten

Beat butter with sugar and lemon rind until light and fluffy. Beat in egg yolks. Stir in lemon juice, flour, cereal and milk. (Mixture will look curdled, but this will not affect finished product.) Fold in beaten egg whites. Pour into greased 1-quart baking dish; place the dish in pan of hot water. Bake at 325° for 1 hour and 15 minutes or until top springs back when lightly touched. When done, pudding has a cake like layer on top with custard below. Serve warm or cold with cream or prepared whipped topping, if desired.

Makes 6 servings.

For individual puddings, pour mixture into five 5-ounce or four 6-ounce custard cups or soufflé cups. Bake for about 40 minutes.

*Or use ½ cup C. W. POST® Hearty Granola Cereal.

EASY VANILLA PUDDING

While mere vanilla pudding may at first seem too plain to be good, this foolproof formula is, in its vanilla-scented purity, delicious. Fortunately for those who demand more than mere vanilla of their puddings, it also comes with two tasty variations.

⅓   cup sugar
¼   cup ARGO® or KINGSFORD'S® Corn Starch
⅛   teaspoon salt
2¾   cups whole or skim milk
2   tablespoons MAZOLA® Margarine
1   teaspoon vanilla

In 2-quart saucepan stir sugar, corn starch and salt. Gradually stir in milk until smooth. Stirring constantly, bring to boil over medium heat and boil 1 minute. Remove from heat. Stir in margarine and vanilla. Pour into serving dish or individual dishes. Cover; refrigerate. Makes about 2½ cups.

EASY BITTERSWEET CHOCOLATE PUDDING: Follow recipe for Easy Vanilla Pudding. Add 1 square (1 oz) unsweetened chocolate, broken in pieces, with milk.

EASY BUTTERSCOTCH PUDDING: Follow recipe for Easy Vanilla Pudding. Substitute ½ cup firmly packed brown sugar for sugar.

MANUFACTURERS' TRADEMARK DECLARATION PAGES

BORDEN, CAMPFIRE, COCO LOPEZ, EAGLE, DREAM WHIP, D-ZERTA and REALIME are registered trademarks of Borden, Inc.

CHIQUITA is a registered trademark of Chiquita Brands, Inc.

M & M's and MILKY WAY Bar are registered trademarks of Mars, Inc.

MARSHMALLOW FLUFF is a registered trademark of Durkee-Mower, Inc. Fluffernutter, © 1961 by Durkee-Mower.

KELLOGG'S, ALL-BRAN, RICE KRISPIES and RICE KRISPIES TREATS are registered trademarks of The Kellogg Company.

BISQUICK is a registered trademark of General Mills, Inc. Recipe reprinted with the permission of General Mills, Inc.

CHEX is a registered trademark of Ralston Purina Company. Traditional Chex® Brand Party Mix© 1989 by Ralston Purina Company. Recipe reprinted with the permission of Checkerboard Kitchens.

HERSHEY'S, REESE'S and REESE'S PIECES are registered trademarks of Hershey Foods corporation. Recipes courtesy of the Hershey Kitchens and reprinted with permission of Hershey Foods Corporation.

NABISCO, NILLA, BLUE BONNET and RITZ are registered trademarks of Nabisco Brands, Inc.

HOT N' SAGEY is a registered trademark of Parks Sausage Company.

LIBBY'S and CARNATION are registered trademarks of The Carnation Company.

PILLSBURY'S BEST, BAKE-OFF and HUNGRY JACK are registered trademarks of the Pillsbury Company.

FRITOS is a registered trademark of Frito-Lay, Inc.

SPAM is a registered trademark for a pork product packed only by Geo. A. Hormel & Company.

QUAKER and AUNT JEMIMA are registered trademarks of The Quaker Oats Company.

ARGO, KINGSFORD, MAZOLA, BEST FOODS, HELLMANN'S, MUELLER'S, SKIPPY, KARO and KNORR are registered trademarks of CPC International and its affiliates. SUPER CHUNK™.

KRAFT, PARKAY, VELVEETA, MIRACLE WHIP, CATALINA, BREAKSTONE'S, BAKER'S, GERMAN'S, JELL-O, COOL WHIP, PHILLY, GRAPE-NUTS, MINUTE RICE, C. W. POST and ANGEL FLAKE are registered trademarks of Kraft General Foods.

OCEAN SPRAY is a registered trademark of Ocean Spray Cranberries, Inc.

SUN-MAID and DIAMOND are registered trademarks of Sun-Diamond Growers.

BLUE DIAMOND is a registered trademark of Blue Diamond Growers. Recipe for Almond Cheddar Pinecone used by permission.

CAMPBELL'S is a registered trademark of The Campbell Soup Company.

LIPTON is a registered trademark of The Thomas J. Lipton Company.

NESTLÉ and TOLL HOUSE are registered trademarks of Nestlé, Inc.

HIDDEN VALLEY RANCH is a registered trademark of HVR Foods.

INDEX